The Christian Young Athlete's Playbook:
101 Bible Devotions and Sports Stories for Tweens & Teens. Build Faith, Discipline & Mental Toughness in Just 3 Minutes a Day

John McKinney

Copyright © 2025 by Kingdom Youth
ISBN: 9798285158158

All rights reserved.

No portion of this book may be reproduced in any form without written permission from the publisher or author, except as permitted by U.S. copyright law.

This publication is designed to provide accurate and authoritative information in regard to the subject matter covered. While the publisher and author have used their best efforts in preparing this book, they make no representations or warranties with respect to the accuracy or completeness of the contents of this book and specifically disclaim any implied warranties of merchantability or fitness for a particular purpose. No warranty may be created or extended by sales representatives or written sales materials. The advice and strategies contained herein may not be suitable for your situation. You should consult with a professional when appropriate. Neither the publisher nor the author shall be liable for any loss of profit or any other commercial damages, including but not limited to special, incidental, consequential, personal, or other damages.

First edition, 2025

CONTENTS

How to Read This Book … 1

Perseverance … 2

Discipline … 14

Courage … 26

Humility … 38

Leadership … 50

Magnanimity … 62

Patience … 74

Teamwork … 86

Gratitude … 98

Integrity Days … 110

How to Read This Book

    Being a successful athlete takes way more than just hard training. In fact, you could argue that practice is important, but it's not the most important part of an athlete's development. What is it then? Ask 100 different athletes and they'll likely give you a similar answer: the secret to success as an athlete is having the right mentality. Talent, effort, practice, having the right coaches, all of these are important things for awn athlete. But without the right mentality, success will be difficult to achieve. The goal of this book is to help you develop a disciplined, perseverant mindset, rooted in faith and biblical wisdom. There are ten sections to this book, each one focusing on a specific virtue that'll help you grow and improve your mentality. In each section, you'll find ten chapters, and in each chapter you'll find:
1. A Bible verse about the specific topic at hand
2. A Real story from a successful athlete to inspire you and to help you learn from their example.
3. Reflection questions and mental exercises for you to start practicing the principles of each chapter in your own life.
4. A short prayer for you to pray and reflect on.
You're supposed to read one chapter every day, which will give you enough time in between chapters to internalize the lessons and put into practice what you're learning. We've written each chapter so that it doesn't take you longer than three minutes to read, so you can make this a daily practice even during periods when you're busy. Finally, once you've read the whole book, feel free to come back to a specific section or a specific day whenever you need to strengthen your mind. The goal of this book is to serve as a resource that you can pick up in the future and find timeless lessons and wisdom to help you through tough times. Throughout the next 101 days, you'll embark on a transformative journey to become not only a better athlete, but also a better Christian, a better leader, and a better person altogether, as you'll develop skills and values that will serve you in all areas of your life.
Keep putting in the work and remember that God is with you every step of the way.

PERSEVERANCE
DAYS 1-10

Day 1
Perseverance Pays Off

"Let us not become weary in doing good, for at the proper time we will reap a harvest if we do not give up."
— Galatians 6:9

BREAKING BARRIERS:
Eliud Kipchoge wasn't always the greatest marathoner alive. After missing Olympic medals and fighting injuries, many would've quit. Not Kipchoge. Through rainy days and under the blazing sun, training in Kenya and crushing defeats, he kept showing up.
"Only the disciplined ones are free in life," he says.
When Kipchoge broke the seemingly impossible two-hour marathon barrier in a special event in 2019, it wasn't just his legs that carried him—it was years of perseverance when nobody was watching. His story teaches us how success eventually comes to those who never stop looking for it, and persevere even when their efforts are not rewarded immediately.

THE GAME PLAN
<u>Reflect</u>
Think about a time you wanted to quit. What kept you going? How did it feel afterward?
<u>Mental exercise</u>
Close your eyes for one minute and imagine pushing through your hardest challenge, feeling both the struggle and the breakthrough.

God, when my muscles ache and I feel unmotivated, remind me that You're building something that takes time. Help me trust Your timing when I want results now. Thank You for promising my effort isn't wasted when I do it for You. Amen.

Day 2
Keep Running the Race

> "Therefore, since we are surrounded by such a great cloud of witnesses, let us throw off everything that hinders and the sin that so easily entangles. And let us run with perseverance the race marked out for us."
> — Hebrews 12:1

LIMPING TOWARD LEGEND:
When Derek Redmond's hamstring snapped during the 1992 Olympic 400-meter semifinal in Barcelona, his dream shattered in an instant. The British runner collapsed, clutching his leg in agony. But something inside wouldn't let him quit. Hobbling and sobbing with each step, Derek struggled forward when suddenly his father burst past security onto the track. "You don't have to do this," his dad whispered. Derek, however, told his dad that he had to finish the race. With the help of his father, he crossed the finish line dead last—yet received a standing ovation that outlasted the winner's celebration. Derek didn't win a medal, but his determination inspired millions to keep running towards the finish line throughout their struggles and pain.

THE GAME PLAN
<u>Reflect</u>
When was the last time you wanted to quit something important? What happened?

<u>Mental exercise</u>
Write down one goal you'll finish no matter what obstacles appear. Post it where you'll see it daily.

Father, when pain makes me want to quit, remind me I'm not running alone, but with You by my side. Give me the courage to keep moving forward, even when victory looks different than I planned. Thank You for running alongside me when I can barely stand. Amen

Day 3
Endurance Through Trials

> "Not only so, but we also glory in our sufferings, because we know that suffering produces perseverance; perseverance, character; and character, hope."
> — Romans 5:3–4

WHEN THE SHARK COULDN'T STEAL HER DREAM:
When 13-year-old Bethany Hamilton paddled out at dawn on October 31, 2003, she had no idea a 14-foot tiger shark would bite off her left arm and cause her severe bleeding. Doctors saved her life, but everyone assumed her surfing dreams were finished. Everyone except Bethany. She refused to let her injury define her future. Just 26 days after the attack, she was back on her board. She taught herself to duck-dive massive waves with one arm and balance differently on her board. Within two years, she won national championships—against competitors with two arms. "I believe in Jesus Christ, and I believe He gave me the passion and determination to continue surfing. You fall off the horse, and you get back on." Bethany says. Her story of faithful endurance remains an inspiring example of perseverance during tough times.

THE GAME PLAN
<u>Reflect</u>
What challenge are you facing that feels impossible to overcome?
<u>Mental exercise</u>
Write down one specific way God might be building your character through this trial.

God, thank You for staying with me in life's toughest waves. When trials knock me down, help me see them as training for something greater. Use my struggles to shape my character and strengthen my hope. Amen.

Day 4
Pushing Past Limits

"Therefore we do not lose heart. Though outwardly we are wasting away, yet inwardly we are being renewed day by day. For our light and momentary troubles are achieving for us an eternal glory that far outweighs them all." — 2 Corinthians 4:16–17

ON THE BRINK OF COLLAPSE:
The night before Game 5 of the 1997 NBA Finals, Michael Jordan was in bed fighting a 103-degree fever. Doctors advised him against playing. But his team needed him with the series tied 2-2.

Jordan staggered onto the court looking pale and weak. Despite needing oxygen during timeouts, he scored 38 points, including the game-winning three-pointer.

After the buzzer, teammate Scottie Pippen had to carry an exhausted Jordan off the court. This event, which became known as the "Flu Game", showed the world that we can find the strength we need within our minds, even if our bodies are hurting.

THE GAME PLAN
<u>Reflect</u>
What's your most common excuse for not giving 100%?
<u>Mental exercise</u>
Choose one situation where you typically back off. Commit to pushing 10% further next time.

Lord, when my body and mind feel weak, renew my spirit. Help me push through temporary struggles and give me courage to take one more step when I want to quit. Thank You for giving me strength beyond my own. Amen.

Day 5
Steadfast and Unshaken

> "Therefore, my dear brothers and sisters, stand firm. Let nothing move you. Always give yourselves fully to the work of the Lord, because you know that your labor in the Lord is not in vain." — 1 Corinthians 15:58

THE SEVENTEEN SECONDS THAT CHANGED HISTORY: The U.S. women's gymnastics team had never won Olympic gold. Everything came down to 18-year-old Kerri Strug's final vault. On her first attempt, she landed poorly and tore some ligaments in her ankle. But she knew that America needed one more solid vault to secure gold. Limping badly, Kerri nodded silently to her coach, determined to win the gold for her country. She then sprinted down the runway on her injured ankle and launched herself into the air. She stuck the landing perfectly on one foot—then immediately collapsed in pain. That vault scored 9.712, enough to secure America's first team gold in women's gymnastics and create one of the Olympics' most iconic moments of determination and perseverance, and steadfastness when it mattered most.

THE GAME PLAN
<u>Reflect</u>
When did you last push through pain because something important was at stake?
<u>Mental exercise</u>
Choose one difficult challenge today and promise yourself: no excuses, no giving up.

Lord, when pain makes me want to stop, help me stand firm. Give me strength to finish what I've started. Help me remember my effort for You is never wasted. Amen.

Day 6
Press On Toward the Goal

"Brothers and sisters, I do not consider myself yet to have taken hold of it. But one thing I do: Forgetting what is behind and straining toward what is ahead, I press on toward the goal to win the prize for which God has called me heavenward in Christ Jesus."
— Philippians 3:13–14

THE 199TH PICK WHO CHANGED FOOTBALL:
At the 2000 NFL Draft, six quarterbacks were chosen before Tom Brady until the Patriots finally selected him 199th overall. He was definitely not someone you'd expect to become one of the greatest quarterbacks of all time.

Brady kept the NFL Combine rejection letter that criticized him. Instead of bitterness and resentment, he used that energy to fuel a mindset of relentless improvement. Years later, after multiple Super Bowl wins, Brady reflected: "I was the kid that was the 199th pick that never had the body for it. People didn't think I'd play one year in the NFL, and now I'm going on my 17th year."

Brady transformed from an overlooked prospect into a 7-time Super Bowl champion and one of the best players ever, largely because of his decision to not let rejection define him

THE GAME PLAN
<u>Reflect</u>
When has someone's doubt fueled your determination?
<u>Mental exercise</u>
Write down one time you've been rejected or disappointed and think about how you can use that to fuel your drive.

Lord, help me stop dwelling on disappointments and press toward what's ahead. When others overlook me, remind me that Your calling matters most. Amen.

Day 7
Overcome the Impossible

"Blessed is the one who perseveres under trial because, having stood the test, that person will receive the crown of life that the Lord has promised to those who love him."
— James 1:12

FROM LEG BRACES TO OLYMPIC GOLD:
At age 4, Wilma Rudolph contracted polio that paralyzed her left leg. Doctors said she would never walk normally again. As the 20th of 22 children in a poor Tennessee family, expensive care wasn't an option. Her mother, however, refused to stop trying to help her daughter get better. Twice weekly, they traveled 50 miles to Nashville for therapy. At home, family members massaged her leg four times daily. By age 12, Wilma was able to remove her metal leg brace and walk unassisted. In high school, she joined the basketball team, before discovering her passion for track. In 1960, the girl who'd once been told she'd never walk again became the first American woman to win three gold medals in a single Olympics. Throughout her life, Wilma credited her mother's unwavering faith and determination as the foundation of her miraculous recovery.

THE GAME PLAN
<u>Reflect</u>
What "impossible" situation are you facing right now?
<u>Mental exercise</u>
Pray for 5 minutes and put that impossible situation into prayer. Give it to God. Use the prayer below for guidance.

Lord, when obstacles seem insurmountable, remind me that You specialize in the impossible. Give me determination to take one step at a time, trusting Your promise of victory. Amen.

Day 8
Find Fuel in Faith

"And as for you, brothers and sisters, never tire of doing what is good."
— 2 Thessalonians 3:13

FROM GROCERY BAGS TO SUPER BOWL MVP:
In 1994, Kurt Warner was stocking shelves at a Hy-Vee grocery store in Cedar Falls, Iowa for $5.50 an hour. Cut from the Green Bay Packers' training camp, he spent nights working and days training, refusing to quit on his NFL dream. Warner played in Arena Football League and NFL Europe before finally getting his chance with the St. Louis Rams in 1999. When starting quarterback Trent Green suffered a season-ending injury, Warner stepped in. That season, he threw for 4,353 yards and 41 touchdowns, was named NFL MVP, and led the Rams to a Super Bowl victory. After the championship game, Warner famously said, "Well, first things first, I've got to thank my Lord and Savior up above — thank you, Jesus!" His journey from grocery bagger to champion quarterback remains one of sports' greatest testimonies of perseverance, faith, and commitment to a dream.

THE GAME PLAN
<u>Reflect</u>
When have you nearly abandoned a dream because progress seemed too slow?
<u>Mental exercise</u>
Write down one dream and three potential setbacks you might face, and three actions you can take to remain persistent.

Lord, when my path seems long and ordinary, remind me You're working behind the scenes. Help me never tire of doing good, even when results aren't immediate. Fuel my persistence with faith in Your perfect timing. Amen.

Day 9
Patience in the Process

> "Be still before the Lord and wait patiently for him; do not fret when people succeed in their ways, when they carry out their wicked schemes."
> — Psalm 37:7

THE PATIENT CHAMPION:

As a child, Naomi Osaka practiced relentlessly against a concrete wall while other kids had proper courts and coaches. Born to a Haitian father and Japanese mother, she moved from Japan to the US at just three years old to pursue her tennis dreams, even though she didn't have the proper resources. For years, she trained and trained, but remained unknown. Even after turning pro at 15, she experienced painful first-round exits which deeply affected her confidence, as she watched peers advance faster.

Her patience paid off in 2018 at the US Open, where she defeated her childhood idol Serena Williams to claim her first Grand Slam title. She went on to win four major championships and become the first Asian player to ever reach #1 in the world rankings. Osaka's journey demonstrates how patience and perseverance through the unseen years of development often precedes public success.

THE GAME PLAN

<u>Reflect</u>

Where are you rushing God's timing in your life right now?

<u>Mental exercise</u>

Identify one area where progress feels too slow and write down the prayer at the end of this chapter. Keep it somewhere you can see it frequently.

Lord, when I want quick results, teach me to trust Your timing. Help me stay faithful during the quiet preparation seasons, knowing You're working even when I can't see it. Give me patience to keep training when progress seems slow. Amen.

Day 10
No Victory Without Perseverance

Pushing through when your legs burn and your lungs scream isn't just about winning games or about earthly victories—it's about building your character. Let's be real: as athletes, we can sometimes obsess over scoreboards and stats. But those wins and records? They're great, but they fade fast.

What sticks with you is who you become in the process—the grit you find when coach makes you run that extra sprint, the character you build when you lose the big game but still show up Monday for practice, and the mental strength you build by getting back up after every failure. That's what matters most. That's what makes a great athlete.

These tough moments aren't just making your body stronger—they're training your heart and soul for life's bigger battles. The Bible puts it clearly: living for God is more a marathon than a sprint. It takes consistency and perseverance, not just random bursts of energy.

Every time you push through pain, every time you get knocked down and stand back up, you're becoming more of who God designed you to be. The medal that really matters isn't hanging in your room—it's the one God's saving for those who keep fighting the good fight of faith. So lace up and keep going. Your best performance is still ahead.

REFLECTION

1. If perseverance were a muscle, how strong would mine be right now? How can I train it better?

2. What story would I want to tell one day about how I stayed faithful when things got tough?

"One More Rep" Challenge:
Choose an area in your training where you're tempted to stop early — whether it's an extra lap, a set of pushups, or a drill. Every time you feel the urge to quit, challenge yourself to do just one more rep, just one more lap. This is a physical way of building perseverance and a reminder that every little bit counts in both your athletic journey and in your walk with God.

Lord, when I want quick results, teach me to trust Your timing. Help me stay faithful during the quiet preparation seasons, knowing You're working even when I can't see it. Give me patience to keep training when progress seems slow. Amen.

DISCIPLINE
DAYS 11-20

Day 11
The Power of Daily Habits

> "Do you not know that in a race all the runners run, but only one gets the prize? Run in such a way as to get the prize. Everyone who competes in the games goes into strict training. They do it to get a crown that will not last, but we do it to get a crown that will last forever."
> — 1 Corinthians 9:24-25

LAST TO LEAVE, FIRST TO ARRIVE:
While his teammates hit the showers, Cristiano Ronaldo stays on the field practicing. While they sleep, he's completing his second workout of the day. CR7's discipline extends beyond practice. Every detail of his life is arranged for maximum performance: He sleeps eight hours every night, he avoids soda and alcohol completely, and even has a personal chef who travels with him.

His former Manchester United teammate Patrice Evra famously said: "I'd recommend nobody to go to his house as he's a machine that doesn't ever stop training."

This unwavering discipline transformed a skinny kid from a poor area of Madeira into arguably the best soccer player in history.

THE GAME PLAN
<u>Reflect</u>
What small daily habit can you start today to grow stronger in faith, mind, or body?
<u>Mental exercise</u>
Set a timer for 10 minutes today and work intentionally on one skill you want to improve.

Lord, thank You for the strength You give me each day. Help me be disciplined in the little things, even when no one sees. Train my heart to honor You in my daily choices. Amen.

Day 12
Mastery Through Routine

"Whoever loves discipline loves knowledge, but whoever hates correction is stupid."
— Proverbs 12:1

6 HOURS DAILY, 6 DAYS WEEKLY, FOR 16 YEARS:
When most kids were playing after school, 6-year-old Simone Biles was already training seriously in gymnastics. At age 14, she was practicing six hours daily, six days every week. Her extraordinary discipline included taking only two vacation days per year. While some of her teammates complained about the repetitive drills, Simone embraced them, allowed herself to be corrected when necessary, and understood that mastery comes through repetition and listening to good feedback. This disciplined approach helped her develop skills so difficult they're even named after her! She's invented five signature moves that push the boundaries of what gymnasts can do. With seven Olympic medals and 30 World Championship medals, Simone's routine-driven excellence has made her the most decorated gymnast in history.

THE GAME PLAN
<u>Reflect</u>
What skill requires your disciplined attention every single day?
<u>Mental exercise</u>
List the top 3 habits or exercises that you should do every single day and commit to making them part of your routine.

Lord, help me embrace correction rather than resist it. Give me strength to stick with important routines even when they're boring or difficult. Like Simone, I want to build excellence through daily discipline. Amen.

Day 13
Small Choices, Big Results

"Whoever can be trusted with very little can also be trusted with much..."
— Luke 16:10

THE 300-SHOT MORNING RITUAL

Before most NBA players even arrive at the arena for practice, Steph Curry has already launched 300 shots. Every. Single. Morning. He follows a precise routine—starting with basic form shots, then adding movement, then game situations. This methodical approach helps him pay attention to even the smallest of details. On Christmas Day 2021, Curry became the all-time NBA leader in three-pointers made. It was historic, and while it might have looked effortless, it was the result of hours and hours of doing the small things right. "I try to make it look easy, but the behind-the-scenes stuff is the challenge," Curry says. Throughout it all, his faith fuels him and keeps him grounded: "In Jesus Name I Play", reads the wristband that he wears during games. His transformation from an undersized college player once considered "too small" for the NBA into a four-time champion proves that small, consistent choices compound into extraordinary results.

THE GAME PLAN

<u>Reflect</u>
What small daily habit can you start today to grow stronger in faith, mind, or body?

<u>Mental exercise</u>
Set a timer for 10 minutes today and work intentionally on one skill you want to improve.

Lord, thank You for the strength You give me each day. Help me be disciplined in the little things, even when no one sees. Train my heart to honor You in my daily choices. Amen.

Day 14
Focus on the Fundamentals

"Whatever you do, work at it with all your heart, as working for the Lord, not for human masters."
— Colossians 3:23

THE BANK SHOT MASTER:
Most NBA stars are always trying to create viral dunks and flashy crossovers. Not Tim Duncan. He decided to become an expert at the basic bank shot—a fundamental skill most players ignore.

For 19 straight seasons with the San Antonio Spurs, Duncan's discipline never wavered. He studied film meticulously, maintained perfect defensive positioning, and performed the same pre-game warmup routine without fail.

Gregg Popovich, his coach, said: "Tim Duncan's the most real, consistent, true person I've ever met in my life." This no-nonsense approach earned Duncan five NBA championships and the nickname "The Big Fundamental." Even after becoming a millionaire and a superstar, Duncan continued arriving early to practice fundamentals that even rookies often consider beneath them. His legacy proves that mastering the basics—not seeking attention—builds lasting excellence.

THE GAME PLAN

<u>Reflect</u>
What fundamental skill in your sport or faith are you tempted to skip?

<u>Mental exercise</u>
Choose one basic technique to practice for 10 minutes daily this week with complete focus.

Father, help me value the fundamentals when I'm tempted to chase only what looks impressive. Teach me that quiet discipline honors You more than public recognition. Remind me that I'm ultimately performing for Your eyes, not for likes or applause. Amen.

Day 15
Training for God's Glory

"For physical training is of some value, but godliness has value for all things, holding promise for both the present life and the life to come."
— 1 Timothy 4:8

SACRIFICE BEYOND THE MAT:

At 14, Gabby Douglas made a difficult decision: to leave her family in Virginia to train with elite coach Liang Chow in Iowa. For two years, she lived with a host family, seeing her mother on only a few occasions during that time. Her training schedule was intensive: 6-hour daily practices, no typical teenage activities, and countless moments of physical pain and homesickness. But throughout her journey, Gabby stayed disciplined and leaned on her faith as her foundation. After making history as the first African American to win Olympic all-around gold in 2012, Gabby pointed upward. When talking about the role that her faith played in her life, she stated: "I give all the glory to God. It's kind of a win-win situation. The glory goes up to Him and the blessings fall down on me."

THE GAME PLAN

<u>Reflect</u>
How could your athletic discipline help strengthen your spiritual discipline?

<u>Mental exercise</u>
Pair each workout this week with a specific spiritual practice (prayer during warmups, gratitude during cooldowns).

Lord, thank You for this body that can train and compete. Help me remember that building character matters more than accumulating medals. May my discipline in sports strengthen my discipline in following You. Let everything I do point to Your glory. Amen.

Day 16
Training for God's Glory

"For the grace of God has appeared that offers salvation to all people. It teaches us to say 'No' to ungodliness and worldly passions, and to live self-controlled, upright and godly lives in this present age."
— Titus 2:11–12

THE DIET THAT CHANGED TENNIS HISTORY:
In 2010, Novak Djokovic was known for his mid-match collapses and breathing difficulties. During crucial moments, he'd suddenly lose energy and forfeit matches or start performing poorly. Everything changed when Dr. Igor Cetojevic discovered Djokovic had severe gluten and dairy sensitivity. Novak immediately eliminated wheat, dairy, and sugar from his diet—a radical change for someone raised on his family's pizza restaurant food. The discipline with which Novak approached this diet was extreme. While competitors enjoyed pasta before matches, Djokovic ate quinoa and vegetables. While they celebrated with champagne, he drank water. Within a year of this dietary discipline, Djokovic won three Grand Slams and became world #1. His 24 Grand Slam titles prove that self-control—saying "no" to certain things—often precedes breakthrough.

THE GAME PLAN
<u>Reflect</u>
What specific food, activity or habit might be holding back your performance?
<u>Mental exercise</u>
Choose one thing to eliminate for 3 days. Notice how it affects your focus and energy.

God, give me strength to say "no" when everyone else says "yes." Help me practice self-control not just for athletic success, but to honor You with my choices. Thank You for showing me that discipline, not overindulgence, leads to freedom. Amen.

Day 17
Sacrifice for the Bigger Goal

"Therefore, I urge you, brothers and sisters, in view of God's mercy, to offer your bodies as a living sacrifice, holy and pleasing to God—this is your true and proper worship."
— Romans 12:1

MAMBA MENTALITY:

Lakers trainer Gary Vitti once arrived at the team facility at 4:15AM. Pretty early right? Well imagine his surprise to find Kobe Bryant already drenched in sweat—he'd started his workout at 3:30.
During the 2012 Olympics, Team USA staff were stunned to discover Kobe had arranged a taxi at 4AM to find an open gym for extra training. Once LeBron James and Dwyane Wade heard about this, they decided to join him. They arrived punctually at 8AM—only to learn Kobe had been up and training since 5Am.
"I'm chasing perfection," Kobe explained. His five NBA championships weren't built on talent alone, but on the uncommon discipline he showed, and on the sacrifices that others weren't willing to make

THE GAME PLAN
<u>Reflect</u>
What sacrifices could you make for the bigger goal ?
<u>Mental exercise</u>
Try to squeeze in a little extra time for training this week. Wake up 30 minutes earlier and practice. You'll notice how it starts to shape your mindset.

Lord, help me see sacrifice as worship—not punishment. Give me courage to choose the difficult path when it leads to growth. Thank You for Jesus' ultimate example of sacrifice. Help me remember that offering my comfort, time, and energy to You is an act of love. Amen.

Day 18
Practicing in the Dark

"But when you pray, go into your room, close the door and pray to your Father, who is unseen. Then your Father, who sees what is done in secret, will reward you."
— Matthew 6:6

BACKUP TO BREAKTHROUGH:

When Jalen Hurts lost his starting quarterback position at Alabama, he had every reason to transfer immediately. Instead, he stayed, trained silently, and humbly supported his replacement.

He was rewarded for this attitude in the 2018 SEC Championship when the starter was injured. Without complaint or rust, Hurts led Alabama to victory. After transferring to Oklahoma, he maintained his discipline of 5AM workouts and late-night film study. Former coaches report he was always first in, last out—even when nobody was watching. This private discipline eventually led Hurts to the NFL's Philadelphia Eagles and Super Bowl LVII. His journey proves that what you do in darkness determines what you'll do in the spotlight. His story is one of quiet, consistent, faithful discipline. As Hurts says: "I've been blessed to grow, learn things, and just mature. And I know God has been there the whole entire way."

THE GAME PLAN

Reflect
Do you work differently when coaches are watching versus when you're alone?

Mental exercise
This week, work in silence, without posting about it or seeking recognition.

Father, help me value Your approval more than attention from others. Teach me to be faithful when no one is watching. Thank You for seeing every unseen effort I make. Amen.

Day 19
Faithful in Little Things

"'Well done, my good servant!' his master replied. 'Because you have been trustworthy in a very small matter, take charge of ten cities."
— Luke 19:17

THE QUIET GENIUS:
While blessed with natural talent, Lionel Messi's true secret has always been his discipline in the smallest of details and in making the most out of his talents. As a child at Barcelona's academy, coaches noted his obsessive focus on basic skills. Year after year, he perfected simple techniques that others considered beneath them. Even after winning his record eighth Ballon d'Or as the world's best player, Messi maintained the same pre-match routine: early arrival, methodical warmup, and careful nutrition—small disciplines performed with remarkable consistency.

His World Cup victory in 2022 wasn't just talent, but the culmination of thousands of faithful moments no one witnessed. As in Luke 19:17, Messi is the perfect example of one who doesn't just rely on his talents, but uses all the blessings he's been given productively.

THE GAME PLAN
<u>Reflect</u>
What talents has God blessed you with? What are you naturally good at?

<u>Mental exercise</u>
Answer the reflection question and think about how you could be using those talents for the good of your athletic career and for the good of the people around you.starts to shape your mindset.

Lord, help me see sacrifice as worship—not punishment. Give me courage to choose the difficult path when it leads to growth. Thank You for Jesus' ultimate example of sacrifice. Help me remember that offering my comfort, time, and energy to You is an act of love. Amen.

Day 20
Practicing in the Dark

In the stories of the great athletes in the past chapters we can clearly see that discipline is the hidden engine behind every great accomplishment in their life. Talent may open the door, but only discipline keeps it open. For young athletes, it's not the occasional burst of motivation that makes champions—it's the daily decision to show up, train hard, and push through discomfort.

Discipline means saying no to distractions, choosing practice over laziness, and remaining consistent when no one is watching. It's waking up early, eating right, and giving full effort even on days you don't feel like it. This habit of doing what is right, even when it's hard, doesn't just build stronger muscles or faster times—it builds character. It teaches mental toughness, responsibility, and perseverance, virtues which will accompany you in other areas of your life: academics, relationships, faith, and future careers. An undisciplined person may have moments of success, but a disciplined person builds a life of lasting impact. As Scripture reminds us, "No discipline seems pleasant at the time, but painful. Later on, however, it produces a harvest of righteousness" (Hebrews 12:11). If you can master discipline now, as a young athlete, you're not just setting yourself up for victory in sports—you're preparing for victory in life.

REFLECTION

1.
How can you create a daily routine that reflects your commitment to your athletic goals, and what areas of your life could benefit from more discipline?

2.
Think of a time when you overcame a challenge in your training or personal life through discipline. What did you learn from that experience, and how can you apply it to future challenges?

"DISCIPLINE THROUGH FASTING" CHALLENGE:

For one day, practice fasting from something non-essential, like social media, junk food, or distractions. Choose something that you enjoy so that the fast is challenging. Use that time to focus solely on your training, prayer, or reading. This exercise builds mental toughness by training your ability to deny immediate gratification in favor of something greater.

Lord, help me develop the virtue of discipline, to defeat laziness and have the strength to do what's right, even when it's uncomfortable. Give me the mental toughness to keep focused on mastering the fundamentals so that I can truly become great and honor you in everything that I do. Amen.

COURAGE
DAYS 21-30

Day 21
Brave Enough to Begin

"Have I not commanded you? Be strong and courageous. Do not be afraid; do not be discouraged, for the Lord your God will be with you wherever you go." — Joshua 1:9

COURAGE IN CLEATS:

On April 15, 1947, Jackie Robinson trotted onto the field wearing #42. This was an event that shattered baseball's color barrier forever. Brooklyn Dodgers owner Branch Rickey had specifically chosen Jackie not just for his talent, but for his character. "I want a ballplayer with enough guts not to fight back," Rickey told him. It wasn't easy for Robinson. He had to dodge pitches aimed at his head, endure spikings on the basepaths, and deal with hotels that refused him rooms simply because of the color of his skin. Some teammates even threatened to quit rather than play with him. Through it all, Robinson responded with dignity, and he didn't let discrimination stop him from winning Rookie of the Year, later MVP, and eventually entering the Hall of Fame. His quiet courage transformed not just baseball, but America itself.

THE GAME PLAN
Reflect
How could your athletic discipline help strengthen your spiritual discipline?
Mental exercise
Pair each workout this week with a specific spiritual practice (prayer during warmups, gratitude during cooldowns).

Lord, thank You for this body that can train and compete. Help me remember that building character matters more than accumulating medals. May my discipline in sports strengthen my discipline in following You. Let everything I do point to Your glory. Amen.

Day 22
Training for God's Glory

"For the grace of God has appeared that offers salvation to all people. It teaches us to say 'No' to ungodliness and worldly passions, and to live self-controlled, upright and godly lives in this present age."
— Titus 2:11–12

THE DIET THAT CHANGED TENNIS HISTORY:

In 2010, Novak Djokovic was known for his mid-match collapses and breathing difficulties. During crucial moments, he'd suddenly lose energy and forfeit matches or start performing poorly. Everything changed when Dr. Igor Cetojevic discovered Djokovic had severe gluten and dairy sensitivity. Novak immediately eliminated wheat, dairy, and sugar from his diet—a radical change for someone raised on his family's pizza restaurant food. The discipline with which Novak approached this diet was extreme. While competitors enjoyed pasta before matches, Djokovic ate quinoa and vegetables. While they celebrated with champagne, he drank water. Within a year of this dietary discipline, Djokovic won three Grand Slams and became world #1. His 24 Grand Slam titles prove that self-control—saying "no" to certain things—often precedes breakthrough.

THE GAME PLAN

Reflect
What specific food, activity or habit might be holding back your performance?

Mental exercise
Choose one thing to eliminate for 3 days. Notice how it affects your focus and energy.

God, give me strength to say "no" when everyone else says "yes." Help me practice self-control not just for athletic success, but to honor You with my choices. Thank You for showing me that discipline, not overindulgence, leads to freedom. Amen

Day 23
Stand Firm and Strong

> "Be strong in the Lord and in his mighty power."
> — Ephesians 6:10

CHAMPION OUTSIDE THE RING:

In 1967, at the peak of his career, Muhammad Ali received news he had been drafted to fight in Vietnam. Ali refused, explaining that his religious beliefs forbade him from serving. This wasn't an easy choice, because Ali knew the consequences: immediately, boxing authorities stripped him of his title. Courts sentenced him to five years in prison (later overturned) and he was banned from boxing during what should have been his prime years. Despite losing millions in earnings, Ali stood strong, stating that he'd rather "face machine-guns" than betray his beliefs. During the time that he was banned from competing, Ali toured colleges speaking about his convictions while continuing to train. In 1970, he was allowed to fight again, and he returned to eventually reclaim his title against George Foreman, proving that standing on principle, even at great personal cost, requires the deepest kind of strength, and that being true to your beliefs is more important than athletic success.

THE GAME PLAN

Reflect
What pressure are you facing to compromise your values?

Mental exercise
Identify one situation this week where you need to stand firm, and write down how God's strength will help you.

Father, when pressure comes, help me rely on Your strength, not mine. Give me courage to stand firm even when it costs me something. Thank You for the power that comes not from my ability, but from Your presence in me. Amen.

Day 24
Take the Risk

> "For the Spirit God gave us does not make us timid, but gives us power, love and self-discipline."
> — 2 Timothy 1:7

FLYING BACK FROM FAILURE:

In October 2017, just months before the PyeongChang Olympics, snowboarder Shaun White crashed during training in New Zealand. The impact split his face open, requiring 62 stitches and five days in the hospital. Many questioned if the 31-year-old should return to competition after such a brutal accident. For many, it seemed too great a risk. And they had a point. White admitted later: "I have never really had that much blood coming out of me before." Despite this setback, he resumed training with renewed determination. At the Olympics, everything came down to his final run. Under immense pressure, White executed his signature move perfectly, scoring an almost perfect rating to win his third gold medal—the redemption run of a lifetime. His courage wasn't fearlessness, but choosing faith over fear when it mattered most. Despite the fear of getting injured again, White took the risk, and made history.

THE GAME PLAN

Reflect
What fear is stopping you from attempting something meaningful?

Mental exercise
Think about times when injuries and setbacks have made you scared to take risks. Pray the prayer below to ask God for courage.

Father, thank You for giving me power instead of timidity. When risks feel overwhelming, remind me that Your Spirit gives me strength beyond my own. Help me step out in faith today. Amen.

Day 25
Courage Over Comfort

> "Be strong and courageous. Do not be afraid or terrified because of them, for the Lord your God goes with you; he will never leave you nor forsake you."
> — Deuteronomy 31:6

RUNNING ON PRINCIPLE:

When Eric Liddell learned his Olympic 100-meter race was scheduled for Sunday, he faced an impossible choice. As a devout Christian, Liddell was very serious about resting on Sundays. He refused to run, despite being Britain's best hope for gold and facing tremendous pressure from the British Olympic Committee. Liddell, however, found a way to compete without compromising his values: he entered the 400-meter race, which wasn't his specialty. Before the final, an American trainer handed him a note with words from 1 Samuel 2:30: "Those who honor me I will honor." Running somewhat awkwardly due to his inexperience in the 400 meter race, Liddell managed to win gold and set a new world record for the race. Liddell remained a brave, devout Christian and continued to show great courage when he later became a missionary in China, eventually dying in a Japanese internment camp in 1945, unwilling to renounce his faith and his duty to God.

THE GAME PLAN

<u>Reflect</u>

What is the one influence that most tries to get you to compromise your values?

<u>Mental exercise</u>

Identify one particular situation this week where you need to choose principle over popularity.

Lord, give me Eric's courage to stand firm even when the world disagrees. Help me remember You go with me through every difficult choice. Thank You for promising never to leave me when I choose to honor You. Amen.

Day 26
Boldness in Faith

> "Be strong and take heart, all you who hope in the Lord."
> — Psalm 31:24

BOMBING SURVIVOR TO FINISHER:

Rebekah Gregory was just three feet away from the first bomb at the 2013 Boston Marathon. The explosion shattered her left leg so severely that after 17 surgeries, doctors finally had to amputate it below the knee. During her long recovery, Rebekah refused to hide her scars or her faith. "I may have lost a leg, but I've found my purpose," she shared publicly. She called her prosthetic leg "Felicia" and decorated it with a Bible verse, showing the whole world how strong her faith was, even during such a difficult time.

Just two years after the bombing, Rebekah returned to Boston. To run again the race that had cost her a leg! Though she collapsed after running the final 3.2 miles on her prosthetic, she crossed the same finish line where her life had changed forever. "I took my life back today," she wrote afterward, "because evil never wins." Rebekah continues sharing her story, showing that courage means moving forward in faith, not allowing fear or darkness to have the final word.

THE GAME PLAN

Reflect
What painful experience could God transform into purpose in your life?

Mental exercise
Think about a recent difficult situation you've faced, and write down how God could turn that pain into a blessing

Lord, strengthen my heart when circumstances feel overwhelming. Help me find purpose beyond my pain. Thank You that my hope in You gives me courage to face whatever lies ahead. Amen.

Day 27
Sacrifice for the Bigger Goal

"So do not fear, for I am with you; do not be dismayed, for I am your God. I will strengthen you and help you; I will uphold you with my righteous right hand."
— Isaiah 41:10

COMEBACK KING:
In Super Bowl LIV, Patrick Mahomes faced a nightmare scenario. His team was down 20-10 to the 49ers with just 7 minutes left, and to make matters worse, he had already thrown two interceptions under relentless pressure, affecting his confidence.

But against all odds, in those critical moments, he remained remarkably calm, leading three consecutive scoring drives to secure a 31-20 victory and MVP honors.

Throughout his career, Mahomes has credited his faith for his composure under pressure. "My Christian faith plays a role in everything I do," he's stated. His composure in crisis comes from knowing he's not alone in the field or in life's biggest challenges: he knows God is with him, and that gives him all the confidence and courage he needs.

THE GAME PLAN

<u>Reflect</u>
When do you feel most anxious about performing? How might remembering God's presence change that?

<u>Mental exercise</u>
Choose a Bible verse about courage and write it on a small card to keep it in your gear bag this week or on a piece of gear that you use for training.

Lord, thank You, for I know I never face pressure alone. When challenges mount, help me stay composed, remembering You're right beside me. Let my confidence come from Your presence, not just my preparation. Amen.

Day 28
Courageous Commitment

"Be strong and courageous, and do the work. Do not be afraid or discouraged, for the Lord God, my God, is with you. He will not fail you or forsake you until all the work for the service of the temple of the Lord is finished."
— 1 Chronicles 28:20

SKIING THROUGH SCARS:

Skier Lindsey Vonn's body tells the story of her impressive career: her 82 World Cup victories haven't come without a fair share of scars and injuries. Her injury list reads like a medical textbook: ACL tears, MCL tears, tibial plateau fractures, concussions, broken bones, and nerve damage, many of them leaving marks on her body.

In 2013, she crashed so severely that her knee was completely shattered. Yet just 10 months later, she was back winning races. When she tore the same ACL again, she returned once more. "Setbacks motivate me," Vonn explained. Even facing her career-ending injury in 2019, she pushed through pain for one final bronze medal at the World Championships. Her 82 World Cup victories didn't just showcase her talent, they also revealed her uncommon courage and her commitment to her goals.

THE GAME PLAN

Reflect
What difficulty tempts you to abandon your calling?

Mental exercise
List three ways you can recommit to your goal this week despite obstacles.

Lord, when pain and setbacks make me want to quit, remind me of Your faithful presence. Give me courage to stay committed to the work You've called me to do. Thank You for never forsaking me. Amen.

Day 29
Victory Through Integrity

"Be strong and let us fight bravely for our people and the cities of our God. The Lord will do what seems good to him."
— 2 Samuel 10:12

CHAMPION BEYOND THE RING:

Saul "Canelo" Álvarez has been dominating the sport of boxing for years. But more impressive than his fists is the way he's kept his integrity and his faith. Throughout his career, the Mexican superstar has consistently pointed upward after victories, acknowledging God as his foundation. His integrity was widely questioned in 2018 when he tested positive for a banned substance. While many fighters choose to deny responsibility when faced with similar problems, he acknowledged the situation while explaining it resulted from contaminated meat in Mexico, a known issue for athletes from his country. Despite heavy criticism, Canelo remained composed and recommitted to proving himself through actions, by voluntarily enrolling in year-round drug testing to demonstrate his commitment to clean competition. "I have always been a fighter with integrity," Canelo has maintained. His resilience through controversy demonstrates that true champions aren't defined by their perfect records but by how they respond when their character is questioned.

THE GAME PLAN

Reflect
Have you been tempted to compromise your values to get ahead?

Mental exercise
Write down one specific way you could practice integrity this week, even if it costs you something.

Lord, help me fight life's battles with both courage and integrity. When shortcuts tempt me, strengthen my resolve to choose what honors You. Thank You that victory comes not just from winning, but from how I compete. Amen.

Day 30
Bold and Fearless

Daring to be great is an act of courage. Most people –not just in the athletic world– remain mediocre because they simply let fear guide them, instead of having the guts to aspire to be great. But courage is not just the virtue that calls you to take risks and dare to aim higher. Most importantly, courage is what's required to remain true to your values when the world criticizes you or tries to get you to betray them.

In today's world sometimes faith is criticized. Sometimes the people around us won't like our commitment to God and to living according to His Word. Being a Christian is often not the most popular choice. And it'll take tremendous courage to remain faithful even when there are temptations and pressures to betray your values.

In the book of Proverbs, it's clearly stated: "Whoever walks in integrity walks securely, but whoever takes crooked paths will be found out." (Proverbs 10:9). The path to greatness will demand courage and fearlessness, to step up when you're scared, to take the risks necessary for victory, and to remain firm in your beliefs. The good news is that you don't need to rely on your own strength, because God is by your side, helping you and supporting you the entire time.

REFLECTION

1.
What are some situations in your life where you've felt fear or doubt, and how could courage help you take action despite those feelings?

2.
Think of a time when you hesitated to do the right thing. What did you learn from that moment, and how can you prepare yourself to act with courage next time?

THE COURAGEOUS CONVERSATION CHALLENGE:

Identify one difficult conversation you've been avoiding, whether it's with a coach, a teammate, or even a family member. This week, commit to having that conversation with honesty and confidence. Whether it's addressing a conflict, sharing a concern, or asking for help, practice stepping out of your comfort zone and confronting the situation with courage.

Lord, help me develop the virtue of courage, to not let myself be guided by fear but by faith. Prepare me for the challenges I'll face and help me to remain faithful to you even when doing the right thing might seem inconvenient. Amen.

HUMILITY
DAYS 31-40

Day 31
True Greatness Starts Low

"For those who exalt themselves will be humbled, and those who humble themselves will be exalted."
— Matthew 23:12

SELLING SUNGLASSES TO NBA SUPERSTAR:
Before becoming an NBA champion, Giannis Antetokounmpo, nicknamed "The Greek Freak", sold sunglasses and other trinkets in the streets of Athens to help his family survive. As Nigerian immigrants in Greece, his family struggled to make a living, sometimes not even having enough to eat. Even after signing a massive $228 million contract, which was, at the time, the largest in NBA history, Giannis remains remarkably humble. He sends money to family in Greece, drives an economical car, and once tweeted about his excitement trying a smoothie for the first time. After winning his first MVP award, reporters asked about his rise to greatness. Giannis responded: "When you focus on the past, that's your ego. When I focus on the future, that's my pride. I try to focus on the present moment—that's humility." His path from poverty to greatness proves Jesus' words that those who humble themselves will be exalted.

THE GAME PLAN
Reflect
How much of your athletic journey centers on promoting yourself versus serving others?
Mental exercise
Find one way to anonymously help a teammate or classmate this week.

Lord, remind me that true greatness begins with humility. Help me stay grounded regardless of success. Teach me to focus on serving You and others rather than promoting myself. Thank You for exalting those who humble themselves. Amen.

Day 32
Stay Small in Success

> "But when you pray, go into your room, close the door and pray to your Father, who is unseen. Then your Father, who sees what is done in secret, will reward you."
> — Matthew 6:6

BACKUP TO BREAKTHROUGH:

When Jalen Hurts lost his starting quarterback position at Alabama, he had every reason to transfer immediately. Instead, he stayed, trained silently, and humbly supported his replacement.

He was rewarded for this attitude in the 2018 SEC Championship when the starter was injured. Without complaint or rust, Hurts led Alabama to victory. After transferring to Oklahoma, he maintained his discipline of 5AM workouts and late-night film study. Former coaches report he was always first in, last out—even when nobody was watching. This private discipline eventually led Hurts to the NFL's Philadelphia Eagles and Super Bowl LVII. His journey proves that what you do in darkness determines what you'll do in the spotlight. His story is one of quiet, consistent, faithful discipline. As Hurts says: "I've been blessed to grow, learn things, and just mature. And I know God has been there the whole entire way."

THE GAME PLAN

<u>Reflect</u>

Do you work differently when coaches are watching versus when you're alone?

<u>Mental exercise</u>

This week, work in silence, without posting about it or seeking recognition.

Father, help me value Your approval more than attention from others Teach me to be faithful when no one is watching. Thank You for seeing every unseen effort I make. Amen.

Day 33
Give Credit to God

"And whatever you do, whether in word or deed, do it all in the name of the Lord Jesus, giving thanks to God the Father through him."
— Colossians 3:17

THE QUARTERBACK WHO KNEELS:
When Russell Wilson led the Seattle Seahawks to their first-ever Super Bowl victory in 2014, his first response wasn't to celebrate extensively or make it about himself, it was to drop to his knees in prayer. This wasn't just a one-time gesture for the cameras. Throughout his career, Wilson has consistently redirected attention from himself to his faith. After touchdown passes, he points upward. After interviews, he ends with "Go Hawks and God bless." His signature phrase "3:16" on social media references John 3:16. He constantly gives credit to God. Most significantly, Wilson maintains this practice of open faith regardless of outside circumstances. When Seattle lost the following year's championship on a controversial interception, Wilson told reporters: "God is too good all the time, man. Every time." His consistent practice demonstrates that true humility means giving credit to God in both triumphs and disappointments.

THE GAME PLAN
<u>Reflect</u>
Do you acknowledge God publicly in the highs and lows?
<u>Mental exercise</u>
Create a simple gesture or phrase to thank God after your next competition—win or lose.

Father, help me redirect praise to You when the spotlight finds me. I want to point upward, not inward. Whether I succeed or struggle, remind me that everything I have comes from You. May my life give You glory in victory and defeat. Amen.

Day 34
Servant-Hearted Leadership

"For even the Son of Man did not come to be served, but to serve, and to give his life as a ransom for many."
— Mark 10:45

TROPHIES THAT TRANSFORM LIVES:
Tim Tebow is a successful athlete, but his greatest impact comes through service. His foundation hosts "Night to Shine" proms for tens of thousands of people with special needs worldwide, while his hospital in the Philippines treats children who couldn't otherwise afford care. After games, Tebow often visits terminally ill children who've come to see him play. During his Florida Gators days, he famously wore Bible verses on his eye black, bringing millions of online searches for verses like John 3:16. "My No. 1 focus was on my foundation, the Tim Tebow Foundation, to bring faith, hope and love to those needing a brighter day in the darkest hour of need," Tebow explains. His leadership extends beyond sports because he prioritizes serving others over personal recognition. Perhaps most telling: Tebow still personally answers emails from families facing crises, demonstrating that true leadership means getting your hands dirty in service.

THE GAME PLAN
<u>Reflect</u>
Who on your team or family might need encouragement or support right now?
<u>Mental exercise</u>
Perform one small act of service daily this week without telling anyone.

Jesus, You modeled true leadership by washing Your disciples' feet. Help me lead like You, seeking opportunities to serve rather than be served. Show me practical ways to put others' needs before my recognition or comfort. Amen.

Day 35
Play for God's Glory

"Humble yourselves, therefore, under God's mighty hand, that he may lift you up in due time."
— 1 Peter 5:6

BACKUP TO BREAKTHROUGH:

Clayton Kershaw has dominated MLB with multiple awards and some of the best stats in modern baseball. Yet his greatest impact isn't found in his pitching stats or in his athletic success.

In 2011, Kershaw and his wife Ellen founded "Kershaw's Challenge" after visiting Zambia and meeting a young girl with HIV. They've since raised millions to build orphanages in Africa, provide surgeries for children with special needs, and serve communities across the country. Even after his first hard-fought victory of the World Series in 2020, Kershaw maintained perspective: "At the end of the day that's why I play the game, to glorify Him in everything I do and to compete for Him."

Every strikeout he records triggers a donation to his foundation, transforming his athletic achievement into kingdom impact. His humility shows that true greatness comes not from seeking the spotlight, but from using it to glorify something greater.

THE GAME PLAN

Reflect
How could your athletic talents serve a purpose beyond trophies and recognition?

Mental exercise
Write a personal mission statement for your sport that focuses on glorifying God.

Father, help me remember my talents are gifts from You. May I use my platform to point others toward something greater than myself. Teach me that true success comes through humble service. Amen.

Day 36
The Talents You've Been Given

"For who makes you different from anyone else? What do you have that you did not receive? And if you did receive it, why do you boast as though you did not?"
— 1 Corinthians 4:7

THE GIFTED, NOT SELF-MADE, CHAMPION:
Despite winning two Masters green jackets and being known for his impressive 300-yard drives, Bubba Watson isn't one to boast. After his dramatic 2012 Masters win, Watson told reporters through tears: "I never got this far in my dreams."
Watson's social media bio simply reads "Christian. Husband. Daddy. Pro Golfer. Author" in that order, which is a clear insight into his priorities. Even when signing autographs, he often includes Bible references to remind fans about working for the Lord, not for human recognition. His perspective reflects today's verse perfectly: recognizing that his talent, opportunities, and success are gifts received, not achievements earned through his own power.

THE GAME PLAN
Reflect
Which of your abilities do you take personal credit for instead of seeing as gifts?
Mental exercise
List three talents God has given you and how you can use each one to honor Him this week.

Father, everything I have comes from You. Guard my heart against pride when I succeed. Help me point to You, not myself, when others notice my abilities. Thank You for entrusting me with gifts that I didn't earn but only received. Amen.

Day 37
Stay Grounded

> "Humble yourselves before the Lord, and he will lift you up."
> — James 4:10

THE GENTLEMAN CHAMPION:

With 20 Grand Slam titles, Roger Federer could have easily become arrogant. Instead, he became renowned for his exceptional humility and genuine personality. After matches, Federer frequently chose to praise opponents before discussing his own performance. Sometimes during rain delays, while other players retreated to private areas, he stayed on the court chatting with ball kids. At tournaments, staff members consistently reported his kindness toward everyone from janitors to directors.

Even when breaking records, Federer deflected praise to his team, family, and competitors who pushed him. His 2017 Australian Open victory speech exemplified this spirit when he told opponent Rafael Nadal: "Tennis is a tough sport. There are no draws. But if there was, I would have been happy to share this with Rafa tonight."

THE GAME PLAN

Reflect
How do you treat others when you're succeeding? Do you remember those who helped you?

Mental exercise
Each day this week, find someone behind the scenes to thank: equipment managers, janitors, or support staff.

Lord, help me stay grounded when success comes my way. Teach me to treat everyone with respect regardless of their position. When I'm tempted toward pride, remind me to humble myself before You first. Amen.

Day 38
Boast Only in Christ

"Let not the wise boast of their wisdom or the strong boast of their strength or the rich boast of their riches, but let the one who boasts boast about this: that they have the understanding to know me."
— Jeremiah 9:23–24

SELLING SUNGLASSES TO NBA SUPERSTAR:
When backup quarterback Nick Foles stepped in for the injured Carson Wentz late in the 2017 season, few expected him to lead the Philadelphia Eagles to their first Super Bowl victory ever by defeating Tom Brady's Patriots. Foles stood at the Super Bowl MVP podium, and instead of highlighting his improbable journey or spectacular performance, his first words reflected a heart of humility: "Unbelievable. All glory to God."

In post-game interviews, Foles gives God His due, first and foremost, and he's openly shared how his faith sustained him through career struggles and temptations to quit. Foles usually mentions his faith before mentioning anything else, a reflection of where his true identity lies.

THE GAME PLAN
<u>Reflect</u>
What accomplishments are you most tempted to boast about?

<u>Mental exercise</u>
Practice redirecting a compliment you get today or this week by acknowledging God's role in your success.

Lord, help me boast only about knowing You. When success comes, remind me that my identity and worth come from being Yours, not from my achievements. Amen.

Day 39
Quiet Strength

"Be careful not to practice your righteousness in front of others to be seen by them. If you do, you will have no reward from your Father in heaven."
— Matthew 6:1

THE WALK-AWAY WARRIOR:
In August 2019, NFL fans were stunned when Andrew Luck, the Indianapolis Colts' star quarterback, announced his retirement at just 29 years old. In the prime of a brilliant career with potentially hundreds of millions in future earnings, Luck quietly decided to step away.

He didn't retire to get attention or create drama. Quite the opposite. After years of injuries and painful recoveries, he simply chose a life of peace and good health with his family over fame and fortune.

Despite being booed by fans who disagreed with his decision, Luck remained gracious. He didn't seek sympathy or stage a farewell tour. In his understated press conference, he simply expressed gratitude to teammates and the organization. "I haven't been able to live the life I want to live," he explained. This wasn't weakness, but rather strength to choose what truly mattered over what the world expected.

THE GAME PLAN
Reflect
Where might you be chasing approval rather than doing what's right?

Mental exercise
Write down the things that matter the most to you. Are they aligned with God's word? Or are they selfish things that are distracting you from what truly matters?

Father, give me courage to choose what's right over what's popular. Help me serve quietly without needing recognition. Thank You that You see every act done in secret. May I learn to value Your approval above the world's applause. Amen.

Day 40
A Humble Heart

It's said that pride often comes before the fall. And for an athlete, this is very much the case. The world of sports comes with its fair share of opportunities to become prideful and arrogant: with success in sports comes popularity, fame, wealth, and social recognition. These aren't necessarily bad, but they can easily lead you away from God if you let them.

But true greatness is found in humility. The former examples of men and women who've succeeded in the world of sports without ever compromising their values and without ever forgetting to put God first and foremost are proof of that. Those are the athletes that will be remembered, and those are the athletes who leave a positive mark in the world beyond their accomplishments in sports.

God warns us throughout the Bible to be vigilant against pride: "When pride comes, then comes disgrace, but with humility comes wisdom." (Proverbs 11:2). If you forget to be humble, you'll forget to follow and trust Jesus, and you'll only end up hurting yourself and those around you. Work hard, stay humble, and God will take care of the rest.

REFLECTION QUESTIONS

1.
When do you feel the need to prove yourself the most—and how might humility change your approach in those moments?

2.
Do you struggle more with pride when you're winning or when you're losing? What would it look like to remain humble in both?

"SPOTLIGHT SHIFT" CHALLENGE:

Pick a teammate or peer who often goes unnoticed. Make it your mission this week to quietly support, affirm, and build them up—publicly or privately. Shift the spotlight off yourself and onto someone else intentionally, as a way to practice humility in action.

Lord, help me develop the virtue of humility, and to remain vigilant about pride and arrogance. Remind me to always give praise to you instead of myself, and to recognize the talents you've given me as gifts from you and not as of my own doing. Amen.

LEADERSHIP
DAYS 41-50

Day 41
Leading by Example

> "Don't let anyone look down on you because you are young, but set an example for the believers in speech, in conduct, in love, in faith and in purity."
> — 1 Timothy 4:12

THE UNEXPECTED LEADER:

Joe Mazzulla wasn't supposed to be the Boston Celtics' head coach. He didn't have NBA playing experience (like most coaches) or extensive coaching credentials. But what he lacked in résumé, he made up for in character. His players quickly started to respect his authentic leadership style, fueled by his daily practice of Scripture reading and prayer. Being the head coach for the Boston Celtics comes with a lot of media scrutiny and high expectations, which can be distracting and stressful. Mazzulla, however, remains centered by focusing on servant leadership, and on being an example of faith, patience, and other virtues for his players. Mazzulla leads the historic franchise not mainly with motivational speeches but through consistent actions: showing up early, maintaining his composure during pressure, and treating everyone with respect. His 2024 championship proved that leadership isn't about certificates or even experience: it's about setting an example others naturally follow.

THE GAME PLAN

<u>Reflect</u>
Where can you influence others without a title or position?

<u>Mental exercise</u>
Choose one area from today's verse (speech, conduct, love, faith, or purity) to strengthen today.

Lord, help me lead through consistent example, not just words. When others watch me, may they see qualities worth following. Remind me that true influence comes not from position but from character that reflects You. Amen.

Day 42
Lift Others Up

"And let us consider how we may spur one another on toward love and good deeds, not giving up meeting together... but encouraging one another."
— Hebrews 10:24-25

THE ASSIST KING:

Magic Johnson revolutionized basketball not just by scoring a lot of points, but also by trying to assist his teammates and make the whole team better. He was good enough that he could dominate games on his own, but he found greater joy in assisting others.

During the Lakers' "Showtime" era, from the late 1970s to early 1990s, Magic elevated seemingly average players into champions. His leadership was all about connection and chemistry. He studied teammates' strengths, preferences, and even their emotions to know exactly what each needed in crucial moments.

Even through adversity—like when facing serious health problems—Magic turned his platform into opportunity by encouraging others. His leadership transcended basketball because he understood that true greatness comes from lifting those around you, and pushing others towards love and greatness.

THE GAME PLAN

Reflect
Who in your circle needs your "assist" right now to reach their potential?

Mental exercise
Identify one specific team member's strength and find a way to publicly acknowledge it this week.

Father, help me lead by finding joy in others' success more than my own spotlight. Give me wisdom to know when teammates need encouragement, challenge, or patience. Thank You for the privilege of lifting others toward their God-given potential. Amen.

Day 43
Pass the Torch

> "And the things you have heard me say in the presence of many witnesses entrust to reliable people who will also be qualified to teach others."
> — 2 Timothy 2:2

THE MEDAL AND MENTORSHIP CHAMPION:

With 11 Olympic medals, Allyson Felix stands as the most decorated American track and field athlete in history. Yet her greatest impact didn't occur in competition. After becoming a mother in 2018, Felix discovered her sponsor, a large sports apparel brand, planned to pay her 70% less. Instead of accepting this quietly, she spoke out against what she considered to be wrong. She made the choice to courageously risk her career to advocate for maternal protections for female athletes, which led to industry-wide policy changes. Throughout her final competitions, Felix intentionally mentored younger runners like Sydney McLaughlin and Gabby Thomas, sharing wisdom about everything from race strategy to handling media pressure. Felix remains committed to her Christian faith: "I have learned that track doesn't define me. My faith defines me. I'm running because I have been blessed with a gift."

THE GAME PLAN

Reflect
What skills or wisdom could you share with someone younger?

Mental exercise
Identify one person you can mentor this week, even in a small way.

Father, help me see leadership as multiplication, not accumulation. Show me who needs what I've learned, and give me courage to invest in others. Thank You for those who've poured into me. Help me continue that legacy by passing the torch. Amen.

Day 44
Speak Life

> "The tongue has the power of life and death, and those who love it will eat its fruit."
> — Proverbs 18:21

THE CALM COMMANDER:
When the Jacksonville Jaguars faced a 27-point deficit in the 2023 NFL playoffs, quarterback Trevor Lawrence remained composed despite throwing four interceptions in the first half. Instead of panicking, Lawrence gathered his teammates and spoke calmly, telling them that they were going to win. His calm words transformed the team's energy, leading to one of the greatest comebacks in playoff history.

Throughout his entire career, Lawrence has been known for his leadership through steady, purposeful communication. Teammates note how he never throws anyone under the bus in press conferences and consistently redirects praise to others after victories.

Even after difficult losses, Lawrence chooses words that build rather than blame. This discipline in his speech reflects his understanding that a leader's words can either breathe life or spread negativity to the entire culture of the team.

THE GAME PLAN
<u>Reflect</u>
How do your words change when you're under pressure or frustrated?

<u>Mental exercise</u>
Write down three encouraging phrases you can use during your next practice or competition.

Jesus, make me mindful of the power of my words. Help me speak life to teammates when they're discouraged. Give me composure during pressure moments. May my voice be Your instrument for building others up, not tearing them down. Amen.

Day 45
Serve First, Lead Strong

> "Anyone who wants to be first must be the very last, and the servant of all."
> — Mark 9:35

THE HEARTBEAT OF BOSTON:

David Ortiz stepped to the plate after the Boston Marathon bombing in 2013, and delivered more than just a speech. With the city still reeling, Ortiz declared: "This is our city. And nobody's gonna dictate our freedom. Stay strong," rallying an entire community that desperately needed strong leadership. Ortiz's greatest impact came through service. Despite being a superstar, he was known for arriving early to help younger players with batting practice. In the clubhouse, teammates recall how he would personally mentor struggling rookies, often inviting them to dinner to discuss challenges away from team pressure.

His leadership style perfectly exemplified Jesus' teaching: greatness comes through service. During the historic 2004 World Series run that broke Boston's 86-year "curse," Ortiz focused on team success rather than personal glory, supporting his teammates and taking on the pressure himself so those who were nervous could perform better.

THE GAME PLAN

Reflect
How might you take pressure off teammates rather than adding to it?

Mental exercise
Find one specific way to serve someone on your team.

Lord, remind me that true leadership begins with serving others. Help me put the needs of my teammates before my own glory. Give me courage to step up when others need strength, and humility to lift others higher than myself. Amen.

Day 47
Courageous Leadership

> "Be strong and courageous, because you will lead these people to inherit the land I swore to their ancestors to give them."
> — Joshua 1:6

RISING FROM THE RUINS:
In 2011, Derrick Rose became the youngest MVP in NBA history at just 22. Everyone was talking about him and his future seemed bright. But then tragedy struck: a devastating ACL tear in the 2012 playoffs changed everything. He had to have multiple surgeries, faced failed comebacks, and critics declared that his career was over. Rose endured not just physical pain but the mental anguish of watching his dream slip away. Yet through it all, Rose led with quiet determination. "As long as I have my faith in God, I'm good. I know everything else is going to come."
After years of setbacks, Rose dropped 50-points in a game against Utah in 2018. This wasn't just a personal triumph but an inspiration to teammates facing their own struggles. His comeback embodied Joshua's command to be strong and courageous when leading others through difficult terrain. Today, Rose mentors younger players, showing that leadership isn't about avoiding falls, but about rising afterward.

THE GAME PLAN
<u>Reflect</u>
What setback are you currently letting define your story?
<u>Mental exercise</u>
Write down one step you'll take today to move forward despite fear.

Lord, give me courage to lead even when I'm afraid. Help me trust Your plan when my path seems blocked. Use my comeback story to inspire others who need hope. Amen.

Day 47
Lead With Class

"You are the light of the world. A town built on a hill cannot be hidden."
— Matthew 5:14

THE CAPTAIN'S CAPTAIN:
In an era of flashy soccer stars, Carles Puyol stood apart. The long-haired defender captained FC Barcelona through their most successful period, winning six La Liga titles, three Champions League trophies, and other domestic trophies. Yet Puyol's leadership wasn't about statistics but about strong, classy character. When teammates celebrated excessively against rivals, Puyol famously pulled them away, demanding respect. After crucial victories, he often pushed younger players forward to receive recognition instead of himself. His leadership extended beyond gestures. Puyol arrived first for training and left last. During contract negotiations, he told management to prioritize signing others before him. When injuries sidelined him, he attended every practice to support teammates. Former coach Pep Guardiola said: "We couldn't be where we are this season without him." His leadership illuminated everyone around him, just as Jesus described in Matthew 5:14.

THE GAME PLAN
Reflect
When have you had an opportunity to lead but stepped back instead?
Mental exercise
Find one situation this week where you can quietly set an example of classy leadership instead of boasting or excessive pride.

Lord, help me lead with quiet strength rather than flashy words. Make me a light that illuminates others' gifts instead of seeking my own spotlight. May my leadership reflect Your character in everything I do. Amen.

Day 48
Cool Under Pressure

"Cast your cares on the Lord and he will sustain you; he will never let the righteous be shaken."
— Psalm 55:22

THE CALM IN THE STORM:

Fierce winds and towering waves are enough to panic most sailors. Not Ben Ainslie. As Britain's most decorated Olympic sailor with four gold medals, Ainslie's leadership emerges most strongly during chaos.

During the 2013 America's Cup, Ainslie's team faced an 8-1 deficit in a first-to-nine series. The pressure was overwhelming. Yet teammates recall how Ainslie gathered them calmly and gave them hope. His unwavering composure sparked the greatest comeback in the competition's 162-year history.

In Olympic competitions, Ainslie's leadership wasn't about shouting orders but demonstrating quiet confidence. His leadership principle echoes today's verse: cast your cares on something greater than yourself, and you'll remain unshaken when others crumble.

THE GAME PLAN

<u>Reflect</u>
How do you currently respond when pressure mounts in competition?

<u>Mental exercise</u>
During your next high-stress moment, practice taking three deep breaths while silently reciting today's verse.

Father, when pressure builds, help me cast my anxieties on You. May I lead others through storms with calm confidence. Thank You for promising to sustain me when everything feels shaken. Amen.

Day 49
Lead with Wisdom

"The beginning of wisdom is this: Get wisdom. Though it cost all you have, get understanding."
— Proverbs 4:7

THE WISE VETERAN:
When Darren Clarke arrived at the Royal St. George's Golf course for the 2011 Open Championship, few considered the 42-year-old Northern Irishman a serious contender.

But while younger players grew frustrated with the brutal weather conditions, Clarke's experience guided his every decision. His caddie noted how Clarke constantly asked questions about wind direction, green speeds, and potential hazards before each shot. On the final day, with pressure mounting, Clarke maintained his methodical approach. His victory at age 42 demonstrated that leadership on golf's biggest stage isn't about raw talent but about wisdom earned through years of both triumph and disappointment.

THE GAME PLAN
<u>Reflect</u>
When have you made decisions based on emotion rather than wisdom?

<u>Mental exercise</u>
Before your next competition, take a methodical approach: analyze the conditions of the game, and identify potential areas of risk or potential opportunities to perform better.

Father, help me value wisdom above quick results. May I lead with thoughtful decisions rather than impulsive reactions. Thank You for promising wisdom to those who ask. Give me understanding that sees beyond the moment. Amen.

Day 50
If Not You, Who?

The world desperately needs leaders. Not just in sports, but in our families, communities, cities and countries, we can become those virtuous leaders that focus on serving, speaking life, motivating, and guiding others towards a brighter future. Leadership isn't a quality reserved for those who are particularly talented. Anyone can be a leader, if they are courageous enough to put themselves out there and volunteer to be the ones that lead.

Very often we stand still, waiting for someone else to take the initiative and lead. But if we take that approach, that leader we are waiting for might never come. Don't wait for someone else to lead. Instead, choose to be the leader when everyone else seeks to avoid the responsibility that comes with leading. The world needs more young leaders who push others towards good. You can be one of those leaders, and help others become better, follow God faithfully, and pursue greatness in all that they do.

REFLECTION QUESTIONS

1.
Who is someone in your life you consider a true leader, and what qualities make them stand out?

2.
Are you leading by example in how you train, treat others, and live out your faith—even when no one's watching?

"TAKE THE LEAD" CHALLENGE:

This week, intentionally take initiative in one area where others usually wait or follow—whether it's starting warmups early, encouraging a teammate who's down, or organizing a group prayer before a game. Lead without needing a title.

Lord, help me become the leader that others need. Help me develop the courage and wisdom to lead others towards You. Help me avoid the temptation to be prideful and arrogant when in positions of leadership and to remain humble, always remembering that I'm here to share Your light. Amen.

MAGNANIMITY
DAYS 51-60

Day 51
Greatness with Self-Control

> "A man without self-control is like a city broken into and left without walls."
> —Proverbs 25:28

UNDEFEATED SPIRIT:
With 29 wins and no losses, Khabib Nurmagomedov dominated the sport of MMA through his extraordinary self-discipline. He was never one to enjoy the celebrity lifestyle. He didn't drink, almost never went out, and stayed away from controversies. Instead, he maintained a monk-like routine: training multiple times daily, avoiding social media distractions, and honoring his religious practices even during fight preparations. He famously maintained his Ramadan fast during training camps, adjusting his entire schedule around prayer times.

Even after big wins, Khabib didn't flaunt his victories but instead emphasized respect and humility. When his father died in 2020, Khabib retired at his prime, demonstrating that family values meant more than fame, fortune, or wealth. "I don't fight for the money. I fight for my legacy. I fight for history. I fight for my people," Khabib said. His legacy proves that true greatness requires exercising self-control before attempting to conquer your field.

THE GAME PLAN

<u>Reflect</u>
What temporary pleasure are you prioritizing over eternal values?

<u>Mental exercise</u>
Identify one habit keeping you from doing your best. Make a commitment to try to quit it.

Lord, help me train with eternal purpose. Give me strength to master myself and my passions before trying to achieve greatness. May my discipline honor You more than any trophy or recognition ever could. Amen.

Day 52
Platform for God's Glory

"For the Mighty One has done great things for me—holy is his name."
—Luke 1:49

UNDER THE SPOTLIGHT:
Ricardo Kaká, a Ballon d'Or winner in 2007, is the perfect example of using his platform to honor God instead of himself. After scoring crucial goals, he'd raise his hands skyward and reveal an undershirt reading "I belong to Jesus" or "God is faithful." His faith wasn't a reason not to aim for greatness, on the contrary, it was the fuel that kept him pushing forward: "Every opportunity that presents itself, my main objective is to conquer and be victorious." Despite amassing wealth and fame that could have distracted him, Kaká consistently used his platform to redirect attention. He's famously stated: "Even though I am playing against others, and it is important to get there and win, I believe that Jesus is much more important than all of that." Kaká has also demonstrated magnanimity through his charitable works: donating significantly to churches in Brazil and supporting humanitarian causes throughout his country.

His example reminds us that true greatness isn't measured by trophies but by recognizing they're merely platforms for a greater purpose.

THE GAME PLAN
<u>Reflect</u>
What achievement or talent might God want you to use as a platform for Him?
<u>Mental exercise</u>
Create a simple gesture or phrase to redirect glory to God after your next success.

Father help me recognize that any greatness in my life comes from You. When others praise me, give me courage to redirect that praise heavenward. May my successes always point to Your glory. Amen.

Day 53
Aim Higher

"Now to him who is able to do immeasurably more than all we ask or imagine, according to his power that is at work within us."
—Ephesians 3:20

REDEMPTION:
Despite winning 28 Olympic medals, Michael Phelps found himself depressed at his competitive peak. After the 2012 Olympics, he hit rock bottom and contemplated suicide until he found the book "The Purpose Driven Life."

"I thought the world would be better off without me," Phelps admitted. His comeback for the 2016 Olympics wasn't just about wanting to win in sports, but about swimming for a higher purpose, about truly becoming great. After recovering, Phelps began mentoring younger swimmers and advocating for mental health, finding greater fulfillment in helping others than breaking records. True greatness, as Phelps shows, comes not from worldly achievements but from aiming toward something higher than personal glory.

THE GAME PLAN
<u>Reflect</u>
What achievements feel empty without deeper purpose?
<u>Mental exercise</u>
Write down a God-sized dream that scares you but excites you.

Father, help me aim beyond trophies toward Your greater purpose. When success feels hollow, remind me that You designed me for more than achievement. Work through me in ways I can't imagine. Amen.

Day 54
Excellence that Stands Out

"Now Daniel so distinguished himself among the administrators and the satraps by his exceptional qualities that the king planned to set him over the whole kingdom."
—Daniel 6:3

CHAMPION OF CHANGE:
Lewis Hamilton is much more than just a wildly successful Formula 1 driver. He's someone that has always used that excellence to try and change his sport and world.

As the only Black driver in F1 history, Hamilton created the Mission 44 foundation to support underrepresented youth in motorsport. He's pushed his team Mercedes to reduce their carbon footprint and advocated for social causes when many athletes stayed silent. Like Daniel in Babylon, Hamilton's excellence opened doors for influence. When you commit to being great, God will give you opportunities to elicit positive change. Hamilton doesn't just win races, he uses his platform to create a legacy beyond trophies. Both Daniel and Lewis show that excellence can allow you to bring incredible good into the world.

THE GAME PLAN
Reflect
What talent could you develop to excellence that might open doors for positive influence?

Mental exercise
Choose one skill to practice with exceptional effort this week.

Lord, help me develop excellence that distinguishes me. May my achievements not just build my reputation but create opportunities to make a difference for You. Guide me to use any success for something greater than myself. Amen.

Day 55
The Race is Long

"Let us run with perseverance the race marked out for us."
—Hebrews 12:1

THE TOUR CHAMPION:
The Tour de France isn't about momentary excellence or effort: it consists of 21 grueling stages across 2,082 miles of mountains, valleys, and countryside.

In 2018, Tour Champion Geraint Thomas understood the importance of pacing himself. While many cyclists got caught up in chasing quick glory in flashy sprint finishes, Thomas knew when to conserve energy, when to push ahead, and when to support his teammates. Through rain, heat, crashes, and mechanical problems, he maintained steady determination. His victory came after years of being a support rider, basically someone who sacrifices personal glory to help team leaders win. This humility prepared him for his own moment of greatness when it finally arrived.

True greatness in life, like cycling's greatest race, isn't about short bursts of brilliance but sustained faithfulness through every challenge.

THE GAME PLAN
Reflect
Where are you sprinting when you should be pacing for a longer journey?
Mental exercise
Identify one area where you need endurance rather than immediate results.

Lord, teach me to run my life's race with perseverance. Help me stay faithful through every challenge, knowing the journey matters as much as the destination. Give me strength for the long haul. Amen.

Day 56
Humble Yet Fierce

"He has shown you, O mortal, what is good. And what does the Lord require of you? To act justly and to love mercy and to walk humbly with your God."
—Micah 6:8

THE GENTLE CHAMPION:

Jordan Burroughs is considered one of the most dominant wrestlers in the world. He's won 6 World Championships and Olympic gold, but his greatness hasn't led him to be prideful and arrogant: the man with over 200 career victories still helps clean the wrestling mats after practice.

The world of wrestling is often synonymous with trash talking, but not for Burroughs. He chooses to praise opponents instead. When he lost at the 2016 Olympics, he faced the media directly rather than hiding and showed remarkable self-awareness: "I'm not as good as I thought I was." On social media Burroughs posts mostly about faith and family. Despite being one of wrestling's greatest stars, he regularly conducts clinics for young athletes in underserved communities. His life embodies Micah 6:8—acting justly in competition, showing mercy to opponents, and walking humbly despite extraordinary success. True greatness combines fierce determination with genuine humility.

THE GAME PLAN

<u>Reflect</u>
Where might your competitive drive be overshadowing humility?

<u>Mental exercise</u>
After your next achievement, practice giving credit to someone who helped you.

Lord, help me balance fierce determination with genuine humility. Teach me to pursue excellence while remembering that all my abilities come from You. May I walk humbly even when achieving greatly. Amen.

Day 57
Joyful and Reverent

"His pleasure is not in the strength of the horse, nor his delight in the legs of the warrior; the Lord delights in those who fear him, who put their hope in his unfailing love."
—Psalm 147:10-11

LEAPING WITH JOY:

Yulimar Rojas stands out from all other great athletes for her enthusiasm and joy. The Venezuelan triple jumper has dominated her event, setting multiple world records with a contagious enthusiasm that makes even spectators smile.

It's not easy being one of track and field's biggest stars, and it's even more difficult to remain humble and joyful throughout striving for greatness. Her lively character was on display after breaking the world record at the Tokyo Olympics, when she remained grateful and humble even after this amazing accomplishment.

In interviews, she consistently points to God and approaches her achievements with reverence, understanding that her record breaking jumps come from something greater than herself.

Her example reminds us that true greatness combines excellence with gratitude and joy with reverence.

THE GAME PLAN

Reflect
Are you happy when competing? How might joy and reverence transform your approach to competition?

Mental exercise
Before your next competition, practice saying "thank you for the opportunity to compete."

Lord, help me compete with a joyful spirit while maintaining reverent gratitude. Remind me that my abilities are gifts from You, not sources of pride. May my excellence always be wrapped in humility. Amen.

Day 58
Bold and Anchored

> "You make your saving help my shield, and your right hand sustains me; your help has made me great."
> —Psalm 18:35

THE CHAMPION WITH ROOTS:

Claressa Shields' titles speak for themselves: she's the first American boxer to win consecutive Olympic gold medals and the first boxer to hold undisputed titles in two weight classes simultaneously. Needless to say, she's an amazing athlete.

Her boldness in the ring is legendary. "I'm the greatest woman boxer of all time," she declares without hesitation. Yet beneath this confidence lies deep spiritual anchoring.

Shields grew up in poverty in Flint, Michigan, and had to deal with abuse, bullying, and tremendous adversity. She attributes her rise not to her own power but to divine strength: "God wanted me to be a great boxer and to tell my story because it's going to save so many lives." Shields proves it's possible to combine boldness and confidence with a deep spiritual anchoring, echoing today's verse and perfectly recognizing that true greatness comes through God's sustaining hand.

THE GAME PLAN

<u>Reflect</u>
Where might God be calling you to be bolder while staying anchored in Him?

<u>Mental exercise</u>
Before your next challenge, pray Psalm 18:35 and visualize God's hand supporting you.

Lord, help me find courage in knowing You sustain me. Make me bold yet humble, confident yet dependent on You. Thank You for being the true source of any greatness in my life. Amen.

Day 59
Leave a Legacy

> "I have fought the good fight, I have finished the race, I have kept the faith."
> —2 Timothy 4:7

THE GOLDEN EXAMPLE:

Sir Chris Hoy retired from cycling as Britain's most decorated Olympian with six gold medals. Unlike many athletes who hang on for too long, desperately trying to stay relevant, Hoy knew when to step away, announcing his retirement with characteristic humility. "I know it is the right decision," he said simply.

Hoy's legacy extends beyond medals. He established a bicycle company focused on making cycling accessible to children. He's authored children's books encouraging young people to persevere through challenges. And he regularly speaks about mental health in athletics, breaking stigmas by sharing his own struggles with confidence. Hoy's story resonates well with Paul's words in today's verse, recognizing that finishing well matters more than momentary glory. True magnanimity means reaching the end of the line knowing you gave your all, fought the good fight, and kept the faith.

THE GAME PLAN

<u>Reflect</u>
What lasting impact do you want to have beyond your competitive days?

<u>Mental exercise</u>
Think about the moment when you'll retire and think about what you'd want to be remembered for.

Lord, help me fight the good fight and finish strong. May my legacy honor You long after my competitive days end. Amen.

Day 60
Excellence is Your Duty

Excellence is not the same as success. Success is very often measured by worldly achievements: your career, how much money you make, your titles and championships. Excellence is much more than that. Excellence is measured by how well you do even the little things, according to your values and virtues. Excellence is measured by who you are and the values that you live by, not by what you have or what you accomplish.

It's perfectly fine to desire greatness and to strive to be successful, but more important than that is striving for excellence, and seeking to lead a life of virtue and goodness. The beautiful thing about striving for excellence is that worldly success will naturally come as a byproduct of seeking excellence.

Beyond that, excellence is our duty because who we are will either inspire or negatively affect other people. Every person that you share your life with, your friends, your siblings, your parents, your coaches, you will impact in some way. You can either impact them positively through living a life committed to excellence and magnanimity, or impact them negatively by living a life of mediocrity. Excellence is a duty that we all have, and by pursuing it, you'll also achieve greatness and success

REFLECTION QUESTIONS
1.
Are you setting goals that stretch you to grow in virtue and service, or are you settling for what's comfortable?
2.
Do you believe God is calling you to something great—and are you preparing your heart and habits to respond boldly?

"EXCELLENCE IN SMALL DETAILS" CHALLENGE:

This week, do your best in even the smallest of details: make your bed every morning, help your parents around the house, and don't slack off in your practice and studies. By practicing excellence in even the smallest details, you'll be prepared for the larger challenges.

Lord, help me be faithful to you even in the smallest of details. Help me pursue excellence every day so I can bring light into the world. Allow me to become a man of virtue, strong values, and unwavering faith, so I can inspire others to do the same. Amen.

PATIENCE
DAYS 61-70

Day 61
Trust the Process

"Let perseverance finish its work so that you may be mature and complete, not lacking anything."
– James 1:4

THE SLOW-BUILT STRONGMAN:

Tom Stoltman's journey to being "The World's Strongest Man" wasn't easy. His autism made certain social aspects of competition challenging, and while physically strong, it took him a while before he could actually compete at the highest levels.

Many others sought shortcuts, but Stoltman embraced the slow path. Each day brought small, often imperceptible gains that eventually accumulated into championship-level strength. When he failed to win his first World's Strongest Man competition in 2020, he didn't quit—he patiently adjusted his approach and returned to win in 2021, 2022, and 2024, becoming the only Briton to have won three World's Strongest Man titles.

His journey mirrors James 1:4—letting perseverance complete its work produces something far more valuable than rushed results. True patience isn't passive waiting but active trust in the process.

THE GAME PLAN

<u>Reflect</u>
Where are you trying to rush what God is building slowly?

<u>Mental exercise</u>
Choose one goal that you are trying to rush to completion and map out small weekly steps rather than focusing on the end result.

Lord, when progress feels slow, help me trust Your timing. Teach me that patience isn't delay but development. Give me strength to persevere, knowing You're completing an important work in me. Amen.

Day 62
Wait With Purpose

> "The Lord is good to those who wait for Him, to the soul who seeks Him."
> – Lamentations 3:25

A PRODUCTIVE PAUSE:

When Bruce Lee, one of the most famous martial artists in history, suffered a severe back injury in 1970, doctors delivered terrible news: he might never kick again. For a martial artist at his peak, this was some of the worst news he could get.

Instead of rushing recovery or giving up, Lee chose to use this waiting period for other productive endeavors related to his discipline: while physically limited, he developed Jeet Kune Do philosophy, wrote extensively, and deepened his mental training. During this forced pause, Lee created his most influential book, "Tao of Jeet Kune Do," drawing insights he might have missed if constantly in motion. He later returned stronger—not just physically, but philosophically and spiritually. True patience isn't passive waiting but purposeful preparation. Like Bruce Lee, we can use apparent setbacks as opportunities for different kinds of growth.

THE GAME PLAN

Reflect
What current limitation could actually be an opportunity for growth?

Mental exercise
List three ways you can develop mentally or spiritually while waiting for physical progress.

Lord, help me wait actively. When I face delays, show me how to use them purposefully instead of despairing. Thank You for working in my waiting seasons, preparing me for what's ahead. Amen.

Day 63
In the Waiting, Grow

> "Be joyful in hope, patient in affliction, faithful in prayer."
> – Romans 12:12

WATCHING WAVES:
Nazaré, Portugal, is home to monstrous, scary up to 70-foot waves. Kai Lenny doesn't seem to be intimidated by them though: he rides them fearlessly. But before he could ride the biggest waves in the world, he was preparing for years, slowly taking on bigger and bigger challenges, preparing patiently when no one was watching. Such big waves might appear only 5-10 days annually, so Lenny doesn't waste time in between. He cross-trains in multiple water sports, studies weather patterns obsessively, and meticulously maintains his equipment. "Surfing taught me patience in an impatient world," Lenny says. "Mastering the small waves prepares you for the giants." His approach shows how true Romans 12:12 is: we are called to remain joyful in hope of big waves to come, patient through flat spells, and faithful in preparation. The waiting isn't wasted; it's where growth happens. True patience isn't idle anticipation but active preparation during seasons when nothing seems to be happening.

THE GAME PLAN
<u>Reflect</u>
What skills could you develop during your current waiting season?
<u>Mental exercise</u>
Create one small daily preparation habit for the opportunity you're awaiting.

Lord, help me use waiting seasons productively. When progress seems slow, remind me that You're preparing me for waves still forming on the horizon. Teach me to be faithful in quiet seasons. Amen.

Day 64
God's Timing Is Perfect

"There is a time for everything, and a season for every activity under the heavens."
– Ecclesiastes 3:1

ONE-ARMED WARRIOR:
Nick Newell was born with a congenital amputation, his left arm ending just below the elbow. Many told him it was pointless to pursue a career in mixed martial arts and that he should do something else. Despite winning fight after fight in smaller promotions with a remarkable 14-1 record, Newell was repeatedly denied his UFC opportunity. While less accomplished fighters received contracts, he continued training and waiting, sometimes questioning if his moment would ever come. His patience was finally rewarded with an opportunity to fight for the UFC through Dana White's contender series in 2018—much later than his talent warranted but at precisely the right moment for maximum impact. Even though he came up short and didn't earn a UFC contract, this fight still marked a big step in his career: "Even if I lose, as long as I know I gave it everything I had, there's no shame in that," he said. Like Ecclesiastes teaches, everything has its appointed season—including the breakthroughs we've been waiting for.

THE GAME PLAN
<u>Reflect</u>
What dream are you rushing that might need God's perfect timing?
<u>Mental exercise</u>
List three possible reasons why God might be making you wait.

Father, help me trust Your perfect timing. When others get opportunities I'm still waiting for, give me patience to keep preparing faithfully. Thank You that my delays aren't denials—just divine timing. Amen.

Day 65
Steady in Setbacks

"When the time is right, I, the Lord, will make it happen."
— Isaiah 60:22

CLIMBING UNEXPECTEDLY:

Growing up in South Africa, Erin Sterkenburg didn't have access to any elite climbing gyms, specialized coaches, or an established path to the Olympics. While climbers in Europe and America trained in state-of-the-art facilities, she practiced on homemade climbing walls and scattered boulders.

Despite these limitations, she refused to rush her development. When competitions went poorly, she simply returned to training. When resources were scarce, she adapted creatively and did what she could with the resources that she did have, without complaining or losing heart. Eventually, this steady commitment led to a historic achievement, as she became the first South African sport climber to qualify for the Olympics in Tokyo.

Her story reflects Isaiah's promise that God makes things happen at the perfect time according to His infinite wisdom, which is not necessarily our preferred time.

THE GAME PLAN

Reflect
Where might impatience be causing you unnecessary frustration?

Mental exercise
Identify one process or goal where you need to embrace the slow, steady climb rather than seeking shortcuts.

Lord, help me remain steady through setbacks and use the blessings and resources I have instead of comparing my journey to that of others. Give me patience to keep training faithfully, trusting that You will open doors at exactly the right time. Amen.

Day 66
Patient Under Pressure

"Being strengthened with all power according to His glorious might so that you may have great endurance and patience."
– Colossians 1:11

STRONG AND SILENT:

While other weightlifters chase followers, fame, and sponsorships, Ireland's Clarence Kennedy built his strength in near obscurity. Training in a basic garage gym, he became known for the extraordinary lifts that he achieved through years of methodical progression. Kennedy gained a cult following not through self-promotion but when videos of his 270kg (595lb) squat and 185kg (407lb) clean and jerk surfaced online. These lifts, which rivaled Olympic medalists, came from patient dedication few witnessed.

His approach embodies Colossians 1:11—finding strength not in shortcuts but in patient endurance. His story reminds us that patient persistence under pressure produces power beyond what rushed training ever could.

THE GAME PLAN

<u>Reflect</u>
Where have you abandoned consistency for quick results?

<u>Mental exercise</u>
Identify one thing that you do in order to gain recognition, and make a commitment to doing it in secret, in order to improve and not to get likes or followers.

Lord, strengthen me with patience under pressure. Help me value consistent effort over quick results. When progress seems slow, remind me that You're building endurance that lasts. Amen.

Day 67
Keep the Vision

> "For the revelation awaits an appointed time... Though it linger, wait for it; it will certainly come and will not delay."
> –Habakkuk 2:3

TEENAGE TRAILBLAZER:
Sky Brown had Olympic dreams since she was just eight years old. However, her journey to the Olympic podium wasn't quick or easy, and it required extraordinary patience through unexpected challenges. In 2020, she suffered a life-threatening accident that left her with skull fractures. Then, the Tokyo Olympics were postponed, adding another year to her wait. Many teenagers would have abandoned their dream, but Sky, just 12 years old at the time, maintained her vision.

"You're going to slam. You're going to fall. But I like it when I fall, it makes me feel good. It's part of skateboarding," Brown explains. Her patience and resilience paid off when, at just 13, she captured bronze in skateboarding's Olympic debut, becoming Britain's youngest Olympic medalist ever.

Her story embodies Habakkuk's promise that though the vision may linger, it will surely come at its appointed time.

THE GAME PLAN
<u>Reflect</u>
What God-given vision are you tempted to abandon because of delays?

<u>Mental exercise</u>
Write down your long-term goal and three reasons to remain patient in pursuing it.

Father, when my dreams seem distant, help me keep the vision alive. Give me resilience to trust Your timing through setbacks. Thank You that delays aren't denials but preparation for Your perfect time. Amen.

Day 68
Humble Yet Fierce

"You need to persevere so that when you have done the will of God, you will receive what he has promised."
– Hebrews 10:36

PLAYING THE LONG GAME:
Before Arnold Schwarzenegger dominated bodybuilding, Hollywood, and politics, he was just a young Austrian kid with broken English and extremely ambitious dreams. His path required extraordinary patience through years of obscurity. Arnold's greatness came from embracing daily discipline: training six hours daily, eating the same bland meals for years, and facing constant rejection in early acting auditions. He famously sent most of his limited earnings home rather than upgrading his lifestyle.

"Strength does not come from winning. Your struggles develop your strengths. When you go through hardships and decide not to surrender, that is strength," Schwarzenegger observed. His seven Mr. Olympia titles came from his patient persistence in doing the same exercises thousands of times when no one was watching. This endurance carried into every arena of his life, embodying Hebrews 10:36—receiving the promise only after patiently persevering through the will of God.

THE GAME PLAN
<u>Reflect</u>
Where are you skipping necessary repetitions because they seem boring?

<u>Mental exercise</u>
Choose one daily discipline to perform consistently this week without variation.

Lord, give me endurance to embrace the daily grind. Help me persist through slow seasons, knowing they're shaping my character. Thank You that patient perseverance leads to Your promises fulfilled. Amen.

Day 69
Hope that Waits

"But those who hope in the Lord will renew their strength. They will soar on wings like eagles; they will run and not grow weary, they will walk and not be faint."
— Isaiah 40:31

THE PATIENT BREAKER:
B-Boy Victor's rise to breakdancing glory wasn't an overnight sensation. Before winning world championships, he endured years of defeat, criticism, and moments when quitting seemed reasonable. Many dancers chase popular trends for quick recognition, but Victor spent countless hours perfecting fundamentals instead. He repeated the same moves thousands of times until they became uniquely his own. When competitions ended in disappointment, he returned to training rather than giving up.

His journey embodies Isaiah's promise—those who place their hope in something greater find renewed strength to persevere when others grow weary. Victor's patience eventually led to championship titles and respect as one of breaking's most innovative pioneers. True hope isn't wishful thinking but patient confidence that faithful persistence will eventually be rewarded.

THE GAME PLAN
<u>Reflect</u>
Where have you grown impatient with God's timing in your life?
<u>Mental exercise</u>
List three ways your current waiting season might be strengthening you.

Lord, renew my strength when waiting makes me weary. Help me place my hope in You rather than immediate results. Thank You that patient endurance leads to soaring like eagles. Amen.

Day 70
A Time To Wait

Very often we try to demand things from God whenever we want them. But God, as the all-knowing father He is, sometimes calls on us to wait. Even though we might not understand why He's making us wait and asking us to be patient, eventually, it always makes sense, as we look back and see clearly that He was preparing us for something special.

Knowing how to wait is just as important as knowing how to perform. It's not always easy to recognize when it's time to be patient and when it's time to press on full-speed ahead, but that's why we must pray to God for wisdom and discernment constantly, so He can show us, in the depths of our hearts, what it is we should be doing.

As we saw in the previous stories of athletes like Bruce Lee, for example, it's important to remember that sometimes it's during those periods of wait when true growth happens, as we are forced to look at things from a different perspective and even find new, creative ways to develop our skills. There's a time to wait, and with God by your side, it can be a great blessing.

REFLECTION

1.
When things don't go your way—on the field or in life—how do you usually respond? Is it with trust or frustration?

2.
Look back on earlier periods of waiting and ask yourself: What has God been trying to teach you in those seasons of your life?

"PATIENCE TIMELINE" CHALLENGE:

Create a "Patience Timeline": Draw or map out a time in your life when you had to wait for something important (a team position, recovery, improvement, etc.). Then write 2–3 sentences next to each point on the timeline describing what God may have been building in you during the wait.

Lord, give me the wisdom to wait when it's time to wait, and to always trust your divine timing. When things don't happen when I want them to, help me see why. Grant me the patience to remain faithful to you even when I don't understand why it's necessary to wait. Amen.

TEAMWORK
DAYS 71-80

Day 71
Built to Win Together

> "Just as a body, though one, has many parts, but all its many parts form one body, so it is with Christ."
> — 1 Corinthians 12:12

A PERFECT MIDFIELD:

FC Barcelona's historic dominance was special. Even though their squad had many superstars, what made them great was the selfless collaboration of three midfielders who elevated each other's strengths. The midfield of Xavi, Iniesta, and Busquets demonstrated that true greatness comes through connection rather than individual brilliance. While Xavi saw passing lanes others couldn't imagine, Iniesta glided through defenders with balletic grace, and Busquets provided defensive stability, each one playing his role to perfection. None sought headlines. None demanded spotlight. They completed over 80 passes per game to each other, creating a flowing style, known as "tiki-taka", that conquered European football for nearly a decade. Their teamwork came from years of practicing together, knowing each other on a personal level, learning each other's movements, and valuing the group's success above individual recognition. This harmony mirrors Paul's vision of the church: different parts with unique functions, unified in purpose and spirit.

THE GAME PLAN

Reflect
Who on your team possesses strengths that complement your weaknesses?

Mental exercise
Identify someone in your team with whom you could develop a closer relationship and find a time to have a conversation to get to know them better.

Lord, when progress feels slow, help me trust Your timing. Teach me that patience isn't delay but development. Give me strength to persevere, knowing You're completing an important work in me. Amen.

Day 72
One Body, Many Roles

"For just as each of us has one body with many members, and these members do not all have the same function, so in Christ we, though many, form one body, and each member belongs to all the others."
— Romans 12:4-5

PLAYING THE LONG GAME:

New Zealand's All Blacks are the most successful sports team in history with almost an 80% win rate spanning over a century. They have had talented players, sure, but their secret is in their "No one is bigger than the jersey" philosophy. From captain to reserve player, everyone cleans the locker room after matches. Their biggest stars sweep floors alongside rookies.

Their culture reinforces that leadership and service are inseparable. When the legendary Wayne Smith became coach, he insisted that every player learn the names of stadium staff, because everyone's contribution matters. The team operates with distinct roles: forwards securing possession, backs creating scoring opportunities, everyone united by a collective trust that each will execute their specific function. This mirrors Paul's vision in Romans 12, where every member serves a purpose and "belongs to all the others" in mutual honor and interconnection.

THE GAME PLAN

<u>Reflect</u>
How might pride be preventing you from embracing your specific role?

<u>Mental exercise</u>
This week, make it a point to be respectful and thankful to service members.

Father, help me serve humbly in my role while honoring others in theirs. Teach me that true teamwork means valuing every member's contribution. May we function as one body with You as our head. Amen

Day 73
Stronger as One

"Two are better than one, because they have a good return for their labor: If either of them falls down, one can help the other up."
— Ecclesiastes 4:9-10

ULTIMATE UNDERDOGS:

No one expected Greece to win the 2004 European Championship. Their odds of winning were 150-1, they had no superstars, no flashy style, and no tournament success history. What they did have though, was extraordinary teamwork. Coach Otto Rehhagel built a system where every player understood their specific role and executed it with precision. Their defense moved as a single unit, shifting and covering for each other selflessly.

They faced Portugal in the final, a team with global stars like Luís Figo, Deco, Rui Costa, and Cristiano Ronaldo, and against all odds, Greece's synchronized teamwork prevailed against the clearly superior individual talent. Angelos Charisteas, who scored the winning goal for Greece, explained: "The moment is unmatchable. Greece is the best team in Europe." Their victory mirrors Ecclesiastes: by supporting one another, ordinary individuals can achieve extraordinary results.

THE GAME PLAN

Reflect
Where are you trying to succeed through individual effort when teamwork would be more effective?

Mental exercise
Identify one teammate's weakness that you could compensate for with your strength and do it.

Lord, remind me that I'm not meant to succeed alone. Help me value teammates who lift me when I fall and give me courage to support others in their struggles. Thank You for designing us to be stronger together. Amen.

Day 74
Serve One Another

> "You, my brothers and sisters, were called to be free. But do not use your freedom to indulge the flesh; rather, serve one another humbly in love."
> — Galatians 5:13

SIMPLE AND BEAUTIFUL:

The 2014 San Antonio Spurs demolished the star-studded Miami Heat in the NBA Finals through extraordinary selflessness. While other teams focused on individual talent, the Spurs averaged 25.4 assists per game, the most in Finals history.

Their "Beautiful Game" featured constant ball movement until the perfect shot emerged. No player averaged more than 18 points; five different players led the team in scoring throughout the series. Head coach Gregg Popovich built this culture on a simple principle: "It's not about any one person. You've got to get over yourself and realize that it takes a group to get this thing done." Even veterans like Tim Duncan and Manu Ginóbili willingly sacrificed minutes and shots to strengthen the team.

Their championship proved that genuine service to teammates creates something greater than individual excellence ever could.

THE GAME PLAN

<u>Reflect</u>

How might personal ambition be limiting your team's potential?

<u>Mental exercise</u>

In your next game, focus on creating opportunities for teammates rather than yourself.

Lord, teach me to serve others before seeking glory. Help me value my teammates' success as my own. Show me how lifting others creates something beautiful. Amen.

Day 75
Shoulder to Shoulder

"Then make my joy complete by being like-minded, having the same love, being one in spirit and of one mind."
— Philippians 2:2

A 5000-TO-1 MIRACLE:
When recently promoted Leicester City won the 2016 Premier League, bookmakers called it the biggest upset in sports history. The team had 5000-to-1 odds, which meant it was more likely to find Elvis alive!

Their miracle wasn't built on specific star power but on extraordinary unity and loyalty. While wealthy clubs spent hundreds of millions on individual talent, Leicester created something more valuable: absolute togetherness.

Players gathered for team dinners, traveled to away games together, and celebrated each other's successes. When striker Jamie Vardy broke a scoring record, the entire team joined his celebration. When defensive midfielder N'Golo Kanté covered impossible ground, teammates acknowledged his unseen work.

Manager Claudio Ranieri fostered this spirit by reminding players they were "foxes hunting together", not a collection of individual talents but a unified pack.

THE GAME PLAN
<u>Reflect</u>
Do you get happy or jealous for the success of your teammates?

<u>Mental exercise</u>
Find a way to create a more personal bond with your teammates today.

Father, help us become like-minded: unified in purpose and spirit. Show me how to strengthen our team's bonds through humility and mutual support. Amen.

Day 76
Unity in the Fire

"As iron sharpens iron, so one person sharpens another."
— Proverbs 27:17

BREAKING THE DROUGHT:

After 108 years of heartbreaking failures, the Chicago Cubs faced elimination in the 2016 World Series. They were down 3-1 against Cleveland, which, all things considered, would make most teams crumble under the weight of history.

Instead, the Cubs' unity intensified through adversity and they showed a rebellious spirit. During a pivotal rain delay in Game 7's extra innings, outfielder Jason Heyward called a team meeting in a weight room. Rather than panic, he reminded teammates of their season-long journey and collective strength. Minutes later, they scored two runs to secure their first championship since 1908.

"I just had to remind them who we are," Heyward said. Throughout their comeback, different players stepped up: Ben Zobrist's clutch hitting, Aroldis Chapman's pitching, David Ross's veteran leadership, each sharpening the others like iron against iron.

THE GAME PLAN

<u>Reflect</u>
Do difficulties divide your team or strengthen your unity?

<u>Mental exercise</u>
Think of one action you can take to encourage your team during your next challenging moment.

Lord, help me bring unity when pressure builds. Thank You for giving me teammates who sharpen me. May our greatest challenges forge our strongest bonds. Amen.

Day 77
Everyone Has a Role

> "From him the whole body, joined and held together by every supporting ligament, grows and builds itself up in love, as each part does its work."
> — Ephesians 4:16

STRENGTH IN SUPPORT:

When the Golden State Warriors won their 2015 championship, the Finals MVP wasn't the obvious superstar Stephen Curry, but Andre Iguodala, who hadn't started a single game that season until the Finals.

This proved that the Warriors' dynasty wasn't built on stars alone but on role players who embraced their specific functions. Iguodala sacrificed scoring to become an elite defender. Shaun Livingston recovered from a devastating knee injury to provide steady leadership off the bench. Kevon Looney did the unglamorous work of setting screens and rebounding.

Coach Steve Kerr emphasized that championship teams need both stars and those willing to do the unnoticed work. "Everybody matters," Kerr often repeated, whether they played 40 minutes or 4. This teamwork mirrors Paul's vision in Ephesians: a body functions only when each part, however small, performs its unique role.

THE GAME PLAN

<u>Reflect</u>
Are you embracing your current role or resenting it?

<u>Mental exercise</u>
List three ways your specific role strengthens your team, even if it's not the spotlight position.

Lord, help me value my role even when it doesn't receive recognition. Remind me that every part matters in Your body. Give me joy in contributing exactly where You've placed me. Amen.

Day 78
Win as One

"I in them and you in me—so that they may be brought to complete unity. Then the world will know that you sent me..." — John 17:23

BEYOND CHAMPIONS:
South Africa's 2019 Rugby World Cup title transcended sport. As the first Black captain in the Springboks' (South Africa's national Rugby team) 128-year history, Siya Kolisi united his team—and his nation—long divided by apartheid's shadow.

The Springboks' "Stronger Together" motto wasn't just a slogan but their living testimony. Players from vastly different backgrounds, from wealthy suburbs to impoverished townships, became brothers with a shared purpose.

Coach Rassie Erasmus deliberately built this unity, teaching players each other's languages and having them visit one another's communities. "The most important thing is the team. You must know what kind of leaders you have around you," Kolisi stated.

When they defeated England in the final, South Africans of all races celebrated together, a powerful picture of Jesus' prayer for unity that testifies to the world.

THE GAME PLAN

<u>Reflect</u>
What differences on your team could become strengths through unity?

<u>Mental exercise</u>
Learn something meaningful about a teammate from a different background than yours.

Lord, make me a unifier in my team. Help me bridge differences and build genuine connections that reflect Your love. May our unity demonstrate Your power to transform relationships. Amen.

Day 79
Honor the Team

"Consider it pure joy, my brothers and sisters, whenever you face trials of many kinds, because you know that the testing of your faith produces perseverance. Let perseverance finish its work so that you may be mature and complete, not lacking anything."
— James 1:2-4

PERSEVERANCE MAKES CHAMPIONS:
Before Spain dominated the world soccer stage from 2008 until 2012, they were known as underachievers. They had always had talented individual players but had been unable to succeed together. Spain's golden generation faced significant internal challenges. Barcelona and Real Madrid players brought club rivalries into the national team. Different regions of Spain had historical tensions. Stars competed for starting positions.

Coach Vicente del Bosque built unity by emphasizing "La Roja" (The Red, the nickname of Spain's national team due to the color of their shirt) identity above club loyalties. Players like Xavi, Iniesta, and Ramos learned to set aside differences for their shared mission. Their perseverance through these trials created unprecedented success: back-to-back European Championships and a World Cup, becoming the first team ever to achieve this "triple crown."

THE GAME PLAN
<u>Reflect</u>
What team challenge could actually strengthen your unity if embraced properly?

<u>Mental exercise</u>
Identify one tension point in your team and consider how addressing it might build collective strength.

Lord, help me view team challenges as opportunities for growth. Give me perseverance through difficulties and wisdom to honor teammates even amid tensions. May our shared trials forge deeper unity. Amen.

Day 80
Together Through Trials

Even in individual sports, no one ever wins on their own. There's always coaches, service staff, and teammates or friends who you practice with. Success in sports is impossible to accomplish on your own. You will always need the help and support of the men and women on your team. It's important to recognize this in order to foster the virtue of teamwork, and avoid the temptations to make it all about yourself.

It's also much more meaningful to win together, as a team, than to win alone. Winning alone and having the spotlight might be fun in the moment, but after a while, you'll be alone. Winning as a team, however, is not only fun, but also incredibly fulfilling, as you'll not only lift trophies but build long-lasting friendships with those that fought alongside you.

REFLECTION QUESTIONS

1.
When things don't go your way—on the field or in life—how do you usually respond? Is it with trust or frustration?

2.
Look back on earlier periods of waiting and ask yourself: What has God been trying to teach you in those seasons of your life?

"TEAMMATE ENCOURAGEMENT NOTES":

Write a personal note to each of your teammates, highlighting their strengths and how they contribute to the team's success. Deliver one note per week and encourage them to pay it forward.

Lord, help me bring unity to my team, by acknowledging the effort of each member and by having the wisdom to give up the desire for the spotlight for the good of the team. Help me lift others up so we can all rise together instead of fighting for personal success. Amen.

GRATITUDE
DAYS 81-101

Day 81
Thankful Through Trials

> "Enter his gates with thanksgiving and his courts with praise; give thanks to him and praise his name."
> – Psalm 100:4

LIMITLESS:

Kyle Maynard was born with no arms below the elbows and no legs beyond the knees. His condition could have easily led him into bitterness, but instead he found reasons for gratitude.

Despite his limitations, Kyle became an award-winning high school wrestler with 35 victories. He learned to deadlift hundreds of pounds. Without prosthetics or assistance, he crawled to the 19,341-foot summit of Mount Kilimanjaro, an impressive feat for anyone, but even more impressive for someone with his condition. Maynard maintained a spirit of gratitude throughout his entire career.

His perspective embodies Psalm 100's call to enter God's presence with thanksgiving, not because life is perfect, but because gratitude transforms our experience of hardship.

Kyle doesn't practice gratitude when trials end; he chooses it in the middle of the struggle.

THE GAME PLAN

Reflect
What challenge are you facing that contains hidden reasons for gratitude?

Mental exercise
List three specific strengths you've developed through a current difficulty.

Lord, help me approach You with thanksgiving even during trials. Open my eyes to see opportunities where others see obstacles. May I find strength in gratitude rather than self-pity. Amen.

Day 82
Gratitude in the Journey

> "In their hearts humans plan their course, but the Lord establishes their steps."
> – Proverbs 16:9

1% BETTER:
When Chris Nikic completed the Ironman Florida in 2020, he didn't just finish a grueling 140.6-mile race, he shattered the expectations of many who didn't believe he could do it. Why? Chris Nikic was born with Down syndrome.

Chris's approach wasn't focused on the finish line but on improving every day. His training philosophy was simple: "Get 1% better every day." After each small improvement or win, he'd thank his support team.

During the race, Chris stopped to hug his guide Dan and thank him between transitions. Even while battling exhaustion in the final miles, he expressed gratitude to volunteers and spectators cheering him on.

His journey embodied Proverbs 16:9: while he planned his course, God established his steps by providing the right people at the right time.

THE GAME PLAN
<u>Reflect</u>
Who has God strategically placed in your journey that deserves recognition?

<u>Mental exercise</u>
Send a specific message of thanks to someone who's supported your growth this week.

Lord, open my eyes to see the people You've placed around me as gifts. Help me express gratitude not just for achievements but for the journey itself. Thank You for establishing my steps even when I can't see the path ahead. Amen.

Day 83
Eyes on the Giver

"You make known to me the path of life; you will fill me with joy in your presence, with eternal pleasures at your right hand."
— Psalm 16:11

RUNNING WITHOUT FEELING:

When high school runner Kayla Montgomery was diagnosed with multiple sclerosis at 14, doctors told her that running would become impossible. The condition blocks nerve signals, causing her to lose all feeling in her legs when her body temperature rises during races. Kayla decided that her disease would not stop her. Instead, she developed a remarkable partnership with her coach. Without sensation to slow down, she would sprint full-speed until the finish line, then collapse into her coach's waiting arms.

What made Kayla extraordinary wasn't just her state championships, but her perspective: "Instead of letting it stop me from running, I've used it to motivate me to break records."

She embraced each race as a gift rather than focusing on what the disease had taken. Her journey reflects Psalm 16:11—finding joy not in perfect circumstances but in God's presence through every step.

THE GAME PLAN

Reflect
What challenge could become an opportunity for gratitude if viewed differently?

Mental exercise
List three abilities you typically take for granted that deserve thanksgiving.

Father, help me focus on You rather than my circumstances. May I find gratitude even in difficulty. Thank You for making known the path of life and filling me with joy in Your presence. Amen.

Day 84
Gratitude in Action

"Therefore, since we are receiving a kingdom that cannot be shaken, let us be thankful, and so worship God acceptably with reverence and awe."
– Hebrews 12:28

RUNNING WITHOUT LEGS:
Blake Leeper, who was born without legs, wasn't supposed to walk, let alone run. Doctors warned his parents about the fact that their son would face severe limitations ahead.

Yet Blake transformed his challenge into opportunity. With prosthetic blades, he became one of the world's fastest Paralympic sprinters, winning silver and bronze medals at the London Paralympics. He even qualified for the U.S. Olympic Trials against able-bodied athletes.

Blake's gratitude isn't just words—it's action. After races, he often removes his blades to show children with similar conditions what's possible. "The only true disability in life is a bad attitude," Blake claims. His life embodies Hebrews 12:28—expressing thankfulness through worship that honors God and encourages others.

THE GAME PLAN
<u>Reflect</u>
How could you transform a personal challenge into an opportunity to inspire others?
<u>Mental exercise</u>
Identify one tangible way to express your gratitude through action today.

Lord, help me demonstrate gratitude not just through words but through how I live. May I use my unique journey to worship You and inspire others. Thank You for the unshakable kingdom I'm receiving through Christ. Amen.

Day 85
Blessings in Every Season

"I know that there is nothing better for people than to be happy and to do good while they live. That each of them may eat and drink, and find satisfaction in all their toil—this is the gift of God."
– Ecclesiastes 3:12–13

THE BLIND MOUNTAINEER:
Erik Weihenmayer lost his sight at just 13 due to a rare genetic disorder. Few expected him to become one of the most famous American mountaineers.

In 2001, Erik became the first blind person to climb to the summit of Mount Everest. But he didn't stop there. He completed the "Seven Summits", the highest point in each continent. He also founded "No Barriers," an organization helping thousands of people with disabilities embrace adventure.

"People have the inner resources to become anything they want to be. Challenge just becomes the vehicle for tapping into those inner resources," Erik explains. Instead of focusing on what he lost, he expresses gratitude for heightened senses of touch, hearing, and team connection that blindness developed.

THE GAME PLAN
<u>Reflect</u>
What challenge in your current season might actually contain hidden blessings?

<u>Mental exercise</u>
List three specific things you're grateful for that you couldn't experience in a different season of life.

Father, help me find Your gifts in every season. Help me see beyond limitations to the unique blessings each challenge brings. Thank You for working through both mountains and valleys in my journey. Amen.

Day 86
Grace Over Glory

> "But thanks be to God! He gives us the victory through our Lord Jesus Christ."
> – 1 Corinthians 15:57

THE HUMBLE CHAMPION:
When Bryan Clay won Olympic gold in the decathlon at Beijing 2008, earning the title "World's Greatest Athlete," his first response wasn't self-promotion but gratitude.

After ten grueling events spanning two days of competition, Clay pointed skyward. In interviews, he consistently redirected praise: "I was blessed with certain gifts and talents and God gave them to me to be the best person I can be and to have a positive impact on other people."

While other Olympians pursued endorsement deals, Clay focused on Heavenly Treasures, his foundation, helping disadvantaged youth.

His perspective exemplifies Paul's teaching that all victory—athletic or spiritual—comes through Christ, not our own strength.

THE GAME PLAN
<u>Reflect</u>
After successes, do you instinctively claim credit or express gratitude?

<u>Mental exercise</u>
Practice a specific gesture or phrase to acknowledge God after your next achievement.

Father, help me see every victory as Your gift. When I succeed, keep me humble and thankful, pointing to Your grace rather than my glory. Thank You for the ultimate victory through Christ. Amen.

Day 87
Honor the Team

> "Then Jesus looked up and said, 'Father, I thank you that you have heard me.'"
> – John 11:41

PRAISING GOD EARLY:

Before Tori Bowie became an Olympic champion, she faced overwhelming obstacles. Abandoned by her biological parents, raised in foster care, and growing up in Mississippi poverty, her path to success seemed unlikely.

Yet throughout her journey to the 2016 Rio Olympics, Bowie practiced something remarkable: thanking God at all times. Teammates noted how she would pray with gratitude before races, not just after medals were secured.

When she captured gold in the 4x100m relay and individual medals in the 100m and 200m, her celebration wasn't surprised joy but confirmed faith. Her approach mirrors Jesus at Lazarus' tomb, expressing gratitude before the miracle, based on who God is rather than what He gives.

THE GAME PLAN

Reflect
What are you waiting to thank God for only after it happens?

Mental exercise
Before your next competition, spend one minute expressing specific gratitude for God's presence regardless of outcome.

Father, like Jesus at Lazarus' tomb, help me thank You before seeing results. Teach me gratitude based on Your character, not just Your gifts. I praise You now for hearing me, whatever lies ahead. Amen.

Day 88
It Comes From Above

> "You may say to yourself, 'My power and the strength of my hands have produced this wealth for me.' But remember the Lord your God, for it is he who gives you the ability to produce wealth..."
> – Deuteronomy 8:17-18

A RUNNING REFUGEE:

At age six, Lopez Lomong was kidnapped from church by Sudanese militants and held captive. After weeks of imprisonment, he escaped with three older boys, running for multiple days and nights until reaching Kenya, where he spent ten years in a refugee camp, where he discovered that he had a talent for and enjoyed running. Eventually relocated to America, Lopez transformed his survival instinct into athletic excellence, becoming a two-time Olympian representing the USA. In 2008, his fellow athletes selected him as the Olympic flag bearer, which was a very solemn moment: a refugee now leading his adopted nation.

Lopez credits God for his remarkable story of survival: "I do not know how we could run so far and so fast and so long. We did not run with our own strength but with strength from God." His perspective echoes Deuteronomy's warning against forgetting the true source of our abilities.

THE GAME PLAN

Reflect
What skill or opportunity do you take personal credit for that actually came from God?

Mental exercise
List three specific abilities you have and write "Thank You, God" beside each one.

Father, forgive me when I claim credit for gifts You've given. Help me recognize that my abilities come from You. Thank You for providing not only talents but opportunities to use them. Amen.

Day 89
Honor the Team

> "This is the day that the Lord has made; let us rejoice and be glad in it."
> – Psalm 118:24

THE HURDLE OF HEARTBREAK:

When Lolo Jones tripped with one of the final hurdles at the 2008 Olympics, she went from certain gold to seventh place in an instant. The devastation was visible as she collapsed on the track, her lifelong dream shattered in seconds.

What followed surprised many. Rather than bitterness, Jones expressed faith: "I never have prayed to win a gold medal at the Olympics and never will. The Lord is my Shepherd and I shall not want. May His will be done."

This perspective carried Lolo through remarkable resilience, becoming one of few athletes to compete in both Summer and Winter Olympics as she later joined the U.S. bobsled team.

THE GAME PLAN

<u>Reflect</u>

How might focusing on gratitude change your response to disappointment?

<u>Mental exercise</u>

Before tomorrow's practice or competition, recite today's verse regardless of how you feel.

Father, help me find joy through gratitude even when facing disappointment. Thank You for making this day, with all its victories and setbacks. Teach me to rejoice in Your presence more than in perfect outcomes. Amen.

Day 90
Praise The Lord

When you're gasping for air after wind sprints or nursing a tough loss, gratitude might be the last thing on your mind. But thanking God for your abilities (even when they seem lacking) transforms how you compete. Grateful athletes play with freedom instead of fear, seeing opportunities where others see only pressure. Studies show they experience less burnout, recover faster, and stay motivated longer than those caught in comparison traps. Your talent is a gift, not an achievement, and recognizing this turns ordinary practices into worship.

Beyond performance, gratitude shapes character long after your playing days end. While trophies gather dust and records fall, thanking God daily builds an unshakable foundation. When you appreciate teammates instead of comparing yourself to them, you create bonds that survive both wins and losses. When you thank coaches for tough feedback instead of getting defensive, you grow faster. In moments when you feel overlooked, gratitude reminds you of the truth that matters most: your worth comes from being a child of God, not your athletic achievements.

REFLECTION

1.
When was the last time you thanked God for something that didn't go your way, and what did you learn from it?

2.
Who in your athletic journey—coaches, teammates, parents—has supported you most, and how have you shown them gratitude?

GRATITUDE LETTER PROJECT:

Write a heartfelt letter to someone who has helped shape your life as an athlete—this could be a coach, a parent, a teammate, or even a competitor who pushed you to improve. In the letter, be specific about what they did and how it impacted you. Then, give or read it to them in person if possible

Lord, help me maintain a spirit of gratitude throughout the highs and lows of my journey. Remind me to praise you and thank you for the countless blessings you've given me and continue to give me each day, Amen.

INTEGRITY DAYS

DAYS 91-101

Day 91
Character Over Talent

"Whoever walks in integrity walks securely, but whoever takes crooked paths will be found out."
– Proverbs 10:9

THE GENTLEMAN RECEIVER:
Football is a sport often defined by showboating and trash-talking. Larry Fitzgerald stood apart from that definition. The 11-time Pro Bowl receiver was known as much for his character as his spectacular catches.

Instead of dancing in the end zone after scoring, Fitzgerald simply handed the ball to officials. When opponents made hard hits, he helped them up rather than retaliating. During contract negotiations, he represented himself rather than hiring an agent who might use deceptive tactics.

His integrity extended beyond the field. After dropping out of college to enter the NFL, Fitzgerald secretly returned to the University of Phoenix, fulfilling a promise he had made to his mother and completing his degree without publicity or fanfare.

This security that comes from integrity reflects Solomon's wisdom in Proverbs 10:9.

THE GAME PLAN

<u>Reflect</u>
Where might you be compromising character for achievement?

<u>Mental exercise</u>
Identify one situation today where you can choose integrity even if it costs you something.

Lord, help me value who I am becoming more than how I perform. Give me courage to walk the straight path even when crooked shortcuts seem appealing. May my character honor You more than my achievements. Amen.

Day 92
Do Right When It's Hard

"If anyone, then, knows the good they ought to do and doesn't do it, it is sin for them."
— James 4:17

PERSEVERANCE MAKES CHAMPIONS:
When Mariano Rivera took the mound in pressure situations, he showed complete calm. Baseball's greatest relief pitcher never showed anger after giving up crucial hits, never bragged after dominant performances.

Many players used performance-enhancing drugs during baseball's "steroid era," but Rivera relied solely on training hard and sharpening his skills. His integrity extended beyond just avoiding shortcuts; after accidentally hitting batters, he would personally check on their well-being.

In a 19-year career with the Yankees, Rivera was never ejected from a single game despite the high-pressure situations he faced, he never lost his composure and was widely regarded as a gentleman. His uniform number 42 was retired not just for his athletic excellence but for his character. "I don't wait for people to give me respect. I always give them respect," Rivera often said, embodying James 4:17 by consistently doing what was right, not just what was easy.

THE GAME PLAN
Reflect
What right action have you been avoiding because it's difficult?
Mental exercise
Identify one situation today where you can choose integrity even when no one would notice if you didn't.

Lord, give me the quiet strength to do what's right even under pressure. Help me choose integrity when shortcuts seem tempting. May my character honor You more than my achievements. Amen.

Day 93
Honesty Wins

> "The Lord detests lying lips, but he delights in people who are trustworthy."
> — Proverbs 12:22

THROWING TRUTHFULLY:
While many NFL stars carefully and sometimes falsely manage their public image, Peyton Manning chose to build a reputation for honesty instead. When his Indianapolis Colts lost big games, Manning never blamed receivers, protection breakdowns, or coaching calls, but as a true leader, took responsibility himself.

After defeats, he took full ownership. After victories, he redirected praise to teammates and coaches: "It was a great team win." When reporters tried to bait him into criticizing opponents, Manning consistently refused.

His integrity extended beyond interviews and press conferences. During contract negotiations, he once corrected his own agent who had overstated his statistics. When receivers ran incorrect routes, Manning addressed mistakes privately rather than publicly embarrassing teammates. His five MVP awards testify to his talent, but his enduring leadership influence comes from embodying Proverbs 12:22: being trustworthy in both words and actions.

THE GAME PLAN

<u>Reflect</u>
Where have you been tempted to shift blame rather than speak honestly?

<u>Mental exercise</u>
Practice taking full responsibility for one mistake today without qualifying or explaining it away.

Lord, help me speak truth even when it costs me something. Give me courage and integrity to own my mistakes and share credit for successes. May my honesty bring You delight. Amen.

Day 94
Play Fair, Always

"Similarly, anyone who competes as an athlete does not receive the victor's crown except by competing according to the rules."
— 2 Timothy 2:5

THE HONEST COMPETITOR:
During a critical Women's World Cup match, with the score tied and minutes remaining, the ball went out of bounds. The referee initially awarded possession to the U.S. team, but Abby Wambach did something unexpected: she told the referee that the ball had touched her last, which gave possession to the opponent at a pivotal moment.

This wasn't an isolated incident. Throughout her record-breaking career, in which she scored 184 goals for the national team, Wambach consistently chose integrity over advantage. In a sport where nearly all players exaggerate contact to draw fouls, she truly tried to remain on her feet when possible.

Her approach embodied Paul's teaching in 2 Timothy—true victory comes only through honorable competition, not shortcuts or deception.

THE GAME PLAN
<u>Reflect</u>
Where are you tempted to bend rules or exaggerate to gain advantage?

<u>Mental exercise</u>
In your next competition, commit to one specific act of integrity even if it might cost you.

Lord, help me compete with total honesty. Give me courage to choose fairness over advantage and integrity over easy wins. May my character honor You more than any trophy. Amen.

Day 95
Actions Reflect Your Heart

"A good man brings good things out of the good stored up in his heart... For the mouth speaks what the heart is full of."
— Luke 6:45

AN ADMIRAL'S CHARACTER:
When David Robinson joined the San Antonio Spurs, he was already exceptional in many ways: a Naval Academy graduate and military officer before becoming an NBA star. But his most significant impact came through the consistent integrity that he showed, revealing his honest heart. Many athletes get caught up in materialism after becoming successful, but not Robinson. He quietly donated $9 million to found a school in a low-income San Antonio neighborhood. While teammates complained heatedly to the referees, he maintained a respectful approach at all times. When fans sought autographs after losses, he stayed to sign and tried to show a good face despite disappointment. Most revealing was his response to the arrival of the promising rookie Tim Duncan. Rather than feeling threatened by Duncan's talent, Robinson mentored him, willingly sharing the spotlight and eventually championship glory. "Your peers will respect you for your integrity and character, not your possessions," Robinson often said. His life embodied Jesus' teaching that outward actions reflect what fills the heart.

THE GAME PLAN
<u>Reflect</u>
What do your private choices reveal about what truly fills your heart?
<u>Mental exercise</u>
Perform one act of integrity or kindness today that no one will witness or praise.

Lord, fill my heart with Your truth so my actions naturally reflect Your character. Help me live with integrity not for recognition but because it's who You've called me to be. Amen.

Day 98
Keep Your Word

"When a man makes a vow to the Lord or takes an oath to bind himself by a pledge, he shall not break his word. He shall do according to all that proceeds out of his mouth."
— Numbers 30:2

PROMISE KEEPER:
When Drew Brees signed with the New Orleans Saints in 2006, the city was still devastated by Hurricane Katrina. Many questioned his decision, but Brees made a bold promise: "We're going to rebuild together."

Unlike celebrities who make fleeting commitments, Brees kept his word. His foundation contributed significantly to New Orleans schools, parks, and community centers. Whenever he promised to visit children's hospitals, he showed up, and not just for publicity, but for regular, unpublicized visits.

Even in small matters, teammates noted his reliability. If Brees said practice would start at 6 AM, he arrived at 5:30. If he promised to review film with a rookie receiver, he'd be there regardless of how tired he felt.

His character reflects the biblical principle that integrity means following through on commitments, big or small.

THE GAME PLAN
<u>Reflect</u>
Where have you made promises you haven't fully kept?
<u>Mental exercise</u>
Choose one commitment you've delayed fulfilling and take concrete action today.

Lord, make me reliable. Help me follow through on every promise whether to You, my team, or my family. May my dependability reflect Your unchanging faithfulness. Amen.

Day 99
Reputation Before Results

> "A good name is better than precious ointment, and the day of death than the day of birth."
> — Ecclesiastes 7:1

QUIET STRENGTH:

Tony Dungy became the first African American head coach to win a Super Bowl. Throughout his coaching career, he maintained remarkable consistency in his character. He never cursed during games. He didn't throw sideline tantrums. He spoke respectfully about opponents rather than using trash talk to motivate players. Most notably, Dungy refused to compromise his principles for victories. He once cut a talented player despite the team's needs because the athlete repeatedly violated team character standards. His faith was fundamental in remaining firm in his principles: "The best leaders are following Christ. That's the best leader you can follow."

His approach embodied Solomon's wisdom that a good name is more valuable than any temporary success.

THE GAME PLAN

Reflect
What decisions might you make differently if reputation mattered more than results?

Mental exercise
Identify one situation where you can choose character over achievement this week.

Father, help me value my name above my accomplishments. Give me quiet strength to prioritize integrity over immediate success. May I build a legacy of character that honors You long after results are forgotten. Amen.

Day 100
Guard Your Honor

Integrity is mainly about doing the right thing when no one's watching. As an athlete, you'll face countless moments when cutting corners seems harmless: a toe just over the line, an uncalled foul you could deny, or training requirements you could fudge when your coach isn't looking. These small choices might seem insignificant, but they're quietly shaping who you're becoming. The athlete who plays with integrity doesn't need different standards for different audiences because their performance is built on truth, regardless of whether it is in front of crowds or alone in the weight room.

Your integrity as an athlete speaks volumes about your faith. When teammates, coaches and opponents see you refusing to compromise even when it costs you something, they glimpse what following Christ actually means. Long after people forget your stats or highlights, they'll remember if you were someone whose word could be trusted. In a sports culture where winning often excuses questionable behavior, your commitment to compete with honesty becomes a powerful witness. Remember: championships record who won, but integrity reveals who you truly are.

REFLECTION

1.
When was the last time you faced a situation where your integrity was challenged? How did you respond, and what could you do differently next time to stay true to your values?

2.
How does your integrity affect the way others perceive you, and how does it influence your ability to lead and inspire others in your faith and personal life?

INTEGRITY JOURNAL:

Over the next week, keep a journal where you record at least one situation each day where you have the opportunity to practice integrity. Reflect on how you made the choice to stay true to your values, what influenced your decision, and how it impacted the people around you. At the end of the week, look over your entries and evaluate how well you're building a habit of

Father, give me strength to live with integrity when no one is watching. Help me choose what's right over what's easy. May my character in competition honor You more than any trophy could. Remind me that Your approval matters most of all. Amen.

Day 101
God Walks With You

"But seek first the kingdom of God and his righteousness, and all these things will be added to you."
— Matthew 6:33

The single most important thing that you'll want to remember throughout your athletic career —and your life—, is that even when times are tough, when you feel lost or lonely, when things seem to be against you, you are not alone. Faith is a beautiful thing, because it is a constant reminder that we are not here by accident, and that we were created out of love by God, Who has a plan and cares for us.

There will be highs and lows, you'll face challenges, injuries and setbacks, but I encourage you to remember that that's part of the journey. From every setback you can learn, in every detour you can practice trusting God. As you have seen in the previous stories of great athletes throughout multiple eras and across various sports, the world of sports is a testing ground for all the virtues that a Christian should try to live by. Hopefully, you have seen in their examples that it's possible to stay faithful and committed to God even while pursuing success and victory as an athlete.

Every single story you read over the past 100 days can teach you something valuable that will hopefully serve you in your life, beyond the world of sports. Maybe you resonated more with some stories than others, but the most important thing is that by reading about great examples of virtue, you begin to internalize what a life of greatness and commitment to the Christian values looks like, so you can, slowly but surely, start shaping your character in a way that glorifies God.

If you ever need a reminder, or simply want to strengthen a specific virtue, come back to this book and read the relevant stories, so you can find motivation to keep fighting the good fight.Now it's time to go into the world and live by those virtues and values. God is with you throughout it all, remember to put your trust in Him and follow Him faithfully. He'll take care of the rest.

Now go out there and compete, and hopefully win, in the name of Christ. God bless you.

Made in United States
Orlando, FL
11 September 2025